SAWNEY BEAN

Dissecting the Legend of
the Scottish Cannibal

SAWNEY BEAN

Dissecting the Legend of the Scottish Cannibal

BLAINE L. PARDOE

To my wife Cyndi, who accompanied me on my research trip across Scotland in search of the truth about this serial killing family of cannibals. 'Haste Ye Back!'

Fonthill Media Limited
Fonthill Media LLC
www.fonthillmedia.com
office@fonthillmedia.com

First published in the United Kingdom and the United States of America 2015

British Library Cataloguing in Publication Data:
A catalogue record for this book is available from the British Library

Copyright © Blaine L. Pardoe 2015

ISBN 978-1-78155-367-1

The right of Blaine L. Pardoe to be identified as the author of this work has been asserted by him in accordance with the Copyright, Designs and Patents Act 1988.

All rights reserved. No part of this publication may be reproduced, stored in a retrieval system or transmitted in any form or by any means, electronic, mechanical, photocopying, recording or otherwise, without prior permission in writing from Fonthill Media Limited.

Typeset in 10.5pt on 13pt Sabon
Printed and bound in England

Contents

Acknowledgements	6
Prologue	7

PART ONE   THE LEGEND

1.	A Contemporary Retelling of the Legend of Sawney Bean	13
2.	The Origins of the Legend	22
3.	The Legend's Sordid Past	41
4.	The Beans Go Mainstream	77
5.	Fictionalizing Sawney Bean	91

PART TWO   LOCATING THE HISTORY

6.	Which King James?	103
7.	The Cimmerian Den	114
8.	Adopting an English Story for Scottish Lore	118
9.	Was There a Real Alexander Bean?	124

PART THREE   SAWNEY BEAN'S LEGACY

10.	The Folklore Grows	129
11.	The Devil's in the Details	140
12.	On Sawney Bean's Trail	143

Appendices	148
Endnotes	166
Bibliography	173

Acknowledgements

Having researched this book for several years, and having spent considerable time in the Galloway region of Scotland, I am familiar with the area, but am far from being a local history expert. In telling this story for a global audience, I have tried to include the appropriate bits of Scottish history. In doing so, I do not profess that this is a complete retelling of the complex and often convoluted history of that great nation—I have simply tried to distil it to the salient points. Any errors in this book are my own.

Historical context is important in how this story evolved. The Scottish people directly and indirectly altered the face of the world. Sawney Bean and his clan rode coattails through history as accepted folklore.

Except in direct quotations, I have referred to the Bean family with the spelling of 'Bean'. The name has been spelled several different ways by different nationalities. I have not corrected the spelling or grammatical context of the various sources. As I have told my wife, some accounts simply are best read with a Scottish accent in mind. Because this book covers the evolution of the tale of the Beans, multiple versions of the story are presented. Each one has a nuance or twist to it, so the story changes with each retelling.

Finally, I would like to thank the following for their helpful contributions to this project: Mairi Hunter, Reference and Local Studies, Dumfries and Galloway Libraries, Information and Archives, Ewart Library; Ann Robson of the Culpeper County Library; Tom Barclay, Reference & Local History Librarian, South Ayrshire Libraries; the Stewartry Museum; Joanne Turner, Museums Officer, Collections, (East) Dumfries Museum and Camera Obscura; Gina Young, Museums Officer, Collections, (West) Stranraer Museum Store & Offices; Graham Stewart, Special Collections Assistant, National Library of Scotland; Alison Gibson, Reprographics Operator, National Library of Scotland; The Scottish National Register; Natalie Rowan, Marketing Executive, The Edinburgh Dungeon, Merlin Entertainments Group; Peter Christie; Moray Teale, Special Collections Assistant, National Library of Scotland; Craig Statham, Local History Officer, East Lothian Library; Peter Locke, Producer of *The Hills Have Eyes*.

Prologue

> Fiend Sawney and his family of cannibals are supposed to have survived for 25 years on the flesh of more than 1,000 innocents they murdered and butchered. Legend says they carved the bodies of their victims into quarters and feasted until they were full. The leftovers were pickled and hung up like sides of beef in their seaside cave.[1]

Over the years, several people have suggested that I look into writing a book about Sawney Bean and his infamous family of cannibal killers. I profess that the first time I heard his name I had no idea who Sawney Bean was. Like many people I turned to the internet to see what I could find out.

The story that was available online was incredible, but then again, many things on the internet are larger than life. The story appealed to me on several levels. One was the scale of the crimes that the Bean family allegedly committed. If one was to believe the legend, the Bean clan was responsible for the murder of over a thousand people. The sheer scope of this would have made Sawney Bean one of the most prolific serial killers in the history of mankind.

Other tantalizing pieces of information made the story unique. This was not just a large-scale murder over decades: it involved cannibalism. The Bean family supposedly not only killed their hapless victims, but feasted on their remains—in fact, that was *why* their alleged victims were slaughtered in the first place.

It was a story of incest as well. Not only did Sawney and his wife live in a cave, but they fostered children, and grandchildren, all through incest. The Beans, when apprehended, were burned at the stake—a fate often befalling witches in this period. This fact alone seems to marry their activities with those of the supernatural in the minds of readers.

The tale of the murderous family is one riddled with intricate details—names of places, approximate dates and times, and a sense of veracity. It

In downtown Dumfries—the author at Sawney Bean's. Word is the finger-food is tasty…

seduces readers into believing the plausibility of the tale, because parts of it are indeed true.

As an award-winning historian and *New York Times* bestselling author of true crime books, it is impossible to not be seduced. The journey took years of research, as I attempted not to prove the legend true or not, but to search for some element of reality. I found people that swear that the story of the Beans is nothing but fiction, the product of an English jab at the Scottish people. I found others that claimed the opposite, pointing to the locales where the horrendous crimes took place and the bits of evidence that can be validated.

A third group of people are unsure. As one woman put it to me, her mother used to use Sawney Bean as a threat ... 'eat your vegetables or Sawney Bean will get you!' Sawney Bean, to some, is akin to the Bogey Man, a horrific mental image to be called upon to intimidate and correct behaviour.

Most bits of folk-tale or legend, like this story, evolve over time, and such is the case with the Beans. Their story has morphed over the years, with new elements constantly added to it to provide future generations with new layers of intrigue.

Like most folklore, the serial killings of the Bean clan have been retold in new mediums. There have been songs about the murdering family; a band named after them; themed restaurants and bars bear the Bean name. The story of their murderous rampage has been interpreted in several films—albeit it altered for the viewers—and plays. Novels casting Sawney Bean as the villain first emerged in the nineteenth century, and have continued to appear up until recently. Comic books have been penned about the incestuous family's cannibalistic cravings. There is even a tourist attraction in Edinburgh that features Sawney Bean and his children retelling their story for audiences every day. The internet has encouraged embroideries of the story with curious and even perverted variations in an even wider forum. The business of Sawney Bean is booming like it never has before.

The story of the serial killers on the west coast of Scotland doesn't follow the traditional path of a piece of folklore. Most folklore begins as a local story, which gains credence before a national, and then world audience. The legend of the mass-murdering Beans didn't start in Scotland, but in England, and was only half-heartedly adopted by the locals of Galloway, and even then with tongue-in-cheek. Ultimately, its credibility has become irrelevant: the Beans have served as source material for numerous works, and the truth merely as a sign-post along the way. One of the most challenging things I have tried to do with this book is to track this lore's evolution.

As a character, Sawney lacks depth. We know little of him, other than he was lazy, fell in with a woman of low morals, and was a bloodthirsty mass-murderer. While he robbed his victims, this cannot have been his motivation, since he and his family never spent their gathered hoard. That leaves us with the cannibalism. Unlike groups such as the Donner Party—where eating human flesh was a matter of survival—the Beans did it because they liked it. Sawney represents a malevolence, an evil that defies unravelling.

I wanted to write this story as if it were a traditional true crime book, but it defied that approach. True crime books follow a pattern—a horrific crime, the search for the killers, their apprehension, their trial, and finally the administration of justice. The Beans proved elusive in fitting into this pattern, since their story lacks testimonies, diaries, journals, or other tangible evidence. The crimes—had they occurred—were so grand and numerous, it would have been impossible to convey in a single book. As such, Sawney forced me to approach this book differently.

So why does this story have such long-lasting appeal? Is it morbid curiosity or something more? People have a need to experience fear and the survival of that terror. This is why horror novels and films have such a great following. We *want* to face evil, even if that evil is imaginary. Serial killers fascinate us, and are a booming business for true crime authors. There is something deeply sinister about someone who mass-murders. And there is the cannibalism aspect of the tale, too, which makes people squirm—toss in incest and a King involved in the manhunt, and you have the makings of a compelling story to read.

In researching this book, the historian in me struggled with the task at hand. I was compelled to explore every nuance of the Bean legend, but the crime writer in me treated this as what it was: an alleged string of murders centuries old. I was not the first to undertake this exercise, but I believe my efforts are the most extensive of recent decades. My role in writing this book is to provide you, the reader, with the facts. In the end, you will have to form your own opinions as to the veracity of the Beans' decades-long rampage in southern Scotland. For many, it simply doesn't matter.

Is the Bean saga true? It is potentially rooted in reality. Folklore is like that, with a kernel of the truth often buried deep within. Where the story of the serial-killing Burke and Hare are well documented, there is a noticeable lapse of documentation in the Bean story. Where Sweeny Todd—another killer whose girlfriend served his victims up as food—is fiction, the Beans seem to straddle the worlds of true crime and pure myth. Pundits on both sides of the argument point to the lack of documentation on the Beans in support of their case. On my travels I met people who swore the story was true, and others who simply gave me a wink and chuckle.

In the end, you the reader will have to form your own opinion....

Part One

THE LEGEND

Captain Charles Johnson's most famous illustration of Sawney Bean outside of his cave.

1

A Contemporary Retelling of the Legend of Sawney Bean

> But do not despise the lore that has come down from distant years; for oft it may chance that old wives keep in memory word of things that once were needful for the wise to know.[1]

It only seems fitting that the legend of Sawney Bean and his band of marauders be retold with the contemporary nuances provided, given how this story has evolved over recent decades.

This first account is steeped in tradition and embedded in the folklore of the people of Galloway. While it cannot be fully verified, it is accepted by many as true. And if we accept things to be true, they become just that—true.

The Tale

Angus sat back in the chair and heard the wood creak as he nestled in. He pulled the woollen blanket over his lap and looked into the fireplace, entranced by the flames dancing against the charred darkness in the backdrop. It was autumn, which meant that colder weather was coming. He glanced out the window into the night and saw the limbs of the gnarled oak whip in the brisk winds.

His grandson, Alister, ran into his field of vision from around the chair. 'Gran'pa, I don't wanna eat the greens.' The mention of dinner made Angus pat his stomach once, as if to honour the lamb stew his wife had cooked.

'What did yer grandma say?'

'"Eat them greens or Sawney Bean will get you tonight."' the boy replied.

He felt his jaw tighten for a moment at the mention of Bean, a flash of memory and horror.

'Then eat yer greens lad.'

'Who is Sawney Bean Gran' pa? I asked Gram but she said she wouldn'a talk about it ... that I was too young.'

Too young? Angus looked at the ten year old. *Was the boy?* No. He should know the truth. There were only a few left alive who witnessed it all, and Angus was the last that he knew of. He motioned for Alister to get closer, casting a glance back towards the kitchen. His wife was busy in there, maybe she wouldn't hear. '*I* don't think you're too young. Come close, and I'll tell you who the Beans were.'

The boy's eyes lit up, realizing that his grandfather was about the share with him something—some story, some secret. He moved in close.

'It was some thirty years ago, a little more than that. The coast was a lot different then ... fewer people. For most of my childhood we knew something was wrong, something evil. You could *feel* it in the winds coming off the shore sometimes. People living along the coast or travelling through along the western road disappeared.'

'Disappeared?' the boy asked in a low voice, low enough so that his grandmother could not hear.

'Yes. No trace of them was found either. The Sheriff in Ayr sent out parties searching, but we never found the men, their horses, or any trace of them. People got nervous. We're not talking just a handful of missing people. The numbers were tens, then dozens, eventually hundreds.'

'What happened to them?'

'What happened *indeed* laddie. We didn'a know. Not knowing made things worse. Now and then a fisherman would find a human limb on the coast. They had cutting marks on the bones. Someone had cut off the arms and legs of some of the missing people, and tossed them into the sea.'

The mention of arms and legs drew the boy in closer, his eyes grew even wider. 'Was it this Sawney Bean?'

Angus paused and narrowed his gaze on the boy. 'Do you want to hear the story or not?' Alister nodded nervously.

'Alright then. We didn't know where these had come from. Spies were hired, armed men, and sent posing as traveling merchants, hoping to root out whoever was behind the disappearances. None of them ever encountered anything out of the ordinary. Some searched the coastline, hoping to spot anything or anyone. They never found anything of use, rumours mostly. Whoever was behind all of the disappearances was good at hiding themselves.

'Suspicions turned to the innkeepers. Some innkeepers were known to rob their victims. You've heard your grandma say that you canna trust innkeepers, haven't ya? Word spread in Ayr that maybe some of the less scrupulous innkeeps had killed the people robbing them.'

'Where were the bodies? And why were there arms and legs in the sea?' the boy pressed, in almost a whisper.

'We thought they had buried them far from their inns, where we couldn't find them. And for the arms and legs, well, we didn't know what to make of that.

'Some of the men, well, they took things into their own hands. Men in mobs, warmed with beer or whiskey, are a dangerous combination lad—remember that. Some of the locals, not me or my pa, went out and found some of the innkeepers suspected of the crimes. They hung them high, swinging in the wind.'

'That didn't stop the disappearances, did it?'

'No. Those innkeeps may have been guilty of other crimes, but they were not behind the missing people. People still went a-missing. Everyone in Galloway knew someone who had been lost. I lost a friend—Peter Hare. He went to go fishing on the coast near Girvan then off to meet with some relatives there, but never arrived. People began to leave. Some said we were cursed. Others said there were monsters or demons roaming the lands. All of them had fear. Many packed up and left. If they knew what was behind it all, they could prepare. But it was not knowing—that was what got to them. It ate at them, gnawed at them every day and night.' The memory of Peter Hare suddenly made Angus feel old. The loss of the boy had taken something from him, personally. He drew a long deep sigh, pulling up the blanket an inch higher on his chest.

'Did they find out who was doing it?'

'Aye,' he replied. 'There was a fair at Girvan. Everyone was there—there was safety in numbers. One of the men, Foster Kennedy, he left with his wife Agnes. Everyone liked his branch of the family, not like some of those inland Kennedys. They rode out from the fair on horseback. They were almost to the western road when they were ambushed.'

'Ambushed?'

'Sawney Beane and his family. His name was Alexander but he was called Sawney. We learned later that he came from East Lothian. A foul man at best, a demon at worst. The women folk say he was spawned of the seed of Satan himself. They were wearing clothing that was filthy. There was a pack of them there that night. They surrounded the Kennedys, armed with knives and swords, and Foster struck at them like a summer storm, he did. They pulled his wife Agnes down off of his horse, but Foster fought back. He fired his pistol, winging one of the savages, slashing at several with his sword. He reeled his horse into them, riding two of the men down.'

'How many were there?' Alister asked, his eyes transfixed on Angus's face.

'Hard to say—we think about a dozen, maybe more. Bean's women, his wife and daughters.... They tore into poor Agnes: they ripped at her throat, and Foster said he saw the women lapping at her blood like thirsty dogs. They gutted her right there, tearing into her like a lamb at the butcher's hands.

Foster fought them back hard. They would have gotten him too, but a bunch of us came from the fair and heard the gunshot and the screaming. We came up on them and the pack of beasts fell back into the shadows. We gave them chase but in the woods, at night, well ... we realised we might be playing right into their hands. These were creatures of the darkness and night.

'I came back with the others to where the ambush had taken place. I saw what they had done to poor sweet Agnes Kennedy. They had torn out her entrails and had gnashed at her throat. Blood was everywhere.' He paused for a moment, and caught himself staring off past his grandson into the fire. For a fleeting second he was not in his home—he was a young boy back there, on that night of horror.

'Did you catch 'em Gran' Pa?' The lad's voice stirred him back to the present.

'Not that night,' he said, stirring in his chair. 'A party of the men took Foster to Glasgow to the magistrate. There had been talk of taking him to the Sheriff in Ayr, but there was fear that the band of killers was so large it required the kind of might that only the officials in Glasgow could muster. The pack of killers roamed that coastal road, no point in giving them another chance at murder. They sent for the king, Jamie VI himself. We came home and hunkered down. I remember me own Pa getting his rifle out and making sure his powder was dry. We'd seen enough of the Beans to know it was going to take many men to track and capture them.'

'Did the king come?'

Angus flashed a thin smile. 'That he did. It was the only time I had seen royalty w' me own eyes. His highness came with four hundred mounted men, packs of bloodhounds, and a desire to put this entire matter to an end once and for all. My Pa allowed me to come, to carry forage. He knew that this was something that you only get to see once in a lifetime. Foster Kennedy came and showed his majesty where his beloved had been slain and described the events, all of us told what we witnessed. Parties of thirty men each were sent out looking for these unholy curs, scouring the countryside. But there was no trace of the Beans.'

'Where did they go?'

'We didna know. My Pa and me were part of a group looking along the shoreline, but we found nothing. For two weeks we looked. You would have thought there would have been a lodge or farm where these beasts lived, but we could not find a trace of them. Some of the men thought them fairies or demons. I heard talk in our party that the king might call off the search and those of us from Girvan feared we'd be left to face their evil designs, whatever they were.

'We were down on the coast south of Bennane Head, when word came from the party to the north that the hounds had come across something.

A Contemporary Retelling of the Legend of Sawney Bean 17

We ran and rode up there to the Head and saw the other search parties arriving as well. There was a howling coming from the rock-face. There, in the Head, was a crack in the ground, a cave. If the tide had been up, we would have missed it entirely, the water would have blocked off access to the entrance. King Jamie was there too. The word we got was that they had passed the cave but the hounds had gone into the cave yelping and howling. The King wanted to make sure he had enough men before ordering his troops into that hell-hole.'

'I know that cave. They say it is haunted,' his grandson said.

'I canna speak to that. I will only tell you that I went in there once, that day, and if you'd seen what I had seen, you'd never go into such a place again in your life.'

'What did you see Gran' Pa?' he probed excitedly.

'I saw the soldiers enter. We wondered whether they had been swallowed by the darkness there, they were in there so long—some of the men thought they might have been killed. Then they started coming out—the Bean family. Filthy and stinking, they started out, a long line of them. We saw them all—men, women, children. There wasn't a familiar face among them. Strangers by choice—that's what they were. The bairns were your

The earliest map of the region where the Beans allegedly lived, with no annotation of the cave or the Bean clan. From the *Carricta Meridionalis Map of South Carrick*. (*South Ayshire Libraries*)

age or younger. As it turns out, the Beans had never been to our villages or towns: they had been living in squalor in that dank hole of theirs.

'Sawney came out last, the father of them all. A beast of a man. Hunched over, his hair down to his shoulders and ratted up like a nest of vipers. His face was gaunt, he had dark circles under his eyes. They chained him up quick. He looked old but you could see that he moved like a snake. I remember feeling a chill when his eyes came my way. He may not have been much, but I knew he was a killer as sure as the sun rises.

'His Highness ordered that we all go into the cave. He said that he wanted us to see where they lived, and what had become of their victims. I didn't understand then, but Pa got us to file into line and go into the cave. I saw one of the men coming out, he stopped on the rocks and threw up. I didn't understand until I went into the cave.

'You couldn't see in there. The smoke from the torches made the air sting at your eyes and throat. I had to squeeze through the cracks in the walls, winding my way back behind the other men. We came into a large chamber, a hollow in the rock. What I saw still haunts me on the darkest nights.'

'What was it? What did you see?'

He closed his eyes for a moment and could still see the images etched into his memory. 'First thing I saw was their plunder. Men were digging into it, all over the floor: coins, gold and silver, piles of them; clothes, wraps of woollen; gentlemen's swords, with gilded basket guards; pistols and rifles tossed about, as if they had no value. This was what the Beans had taken from their victims. There was enough treasury there to buy a castle and live like a lord.

'Then ... I saw their harvest along the walls—legs and arms hanging on hooks staked into the stone. Some were blackened from drying out. They ...' he paused, suddenly questioning whether his grandson was old enough to hear what horrors he had seen after all, 'were limbs of men, women—and children.'

'They ... they were hanging them to eat?'

'Cannibals, that's what those bastards were,' he said nodding. 'There were several barrels of brine, where they were pickling human parts. We found crocks sealed with wax filled with the parts of their victims. Sawney and his clan had butchered those they found. That was why we never found them. No one survived a meeting with these hell-hounds. The only time we ever found evidence of them was when a limb went bad and they tossed it into the sea.'

'How could they eat people?'

'They were not human beings: they were monsters, straight out of Satan's realm,' Angus spat back with a sour expression. 'We came back to the entrance and there wasn't a man there that was not shaken by what we had seen. Some called for justice right then and there—burn them like witches at the stake. King Jamie said no. He wanted the rest of the realm to know what had happened, and to see the fate of such men. His Majesty ordered the remains of those poor souls brought out to the sands and buried, with a religious service.'

'Did Sawney Bean talk—why did they do it?'

'The guard was strong around them, out of fear that someone who had lost a loved one to his wretched hand might take revenge. I will tell you there was talk of it, despite the king's orders. I didn't speak to him, but one of the guards said they overheard the king interrogate him.

'He told me that Sawney's family had inbred. He had fathered his own grandchildren. Their brothers and sisters had bred in that cave of theirs, raising children that were bastardised and cursed. That hoard was the product of unholy incest. It would be like you and your sister marrying—wrong in the eyes of men and God alike.'

Alister winced at the suggestion. Angus reached out and put his hand on his grandson's shoulder. 'The horrors of what took place in that cavern was something that was a blight on these Bean's. In the end, we guessed that nearly a thousand men, women, and children had fallen to their bloody hands and were consumed in that black hole in Bennane Head.

'King Jamie sent riders out ahead of us to tell every community that we had apprehended these beasts. When we came to every town and village the people came out to see these criminals. Most threw dung or rotted vegetables at them, spitting on them, and casting rocks. The Beans were not pennant in the least; they cursed and spat back at the people that called on them to die. I didn't go, but me Pa did. He said it was nearly a riot in Glasgow when they came in, so many were the people crying for justice. If it had not been for his majesty himself ordering calm, the Beans would have died there.'

'Did he imprison them?'

'No. He took them on to Edinburgh. They were locked away in the Tolbooth there. But it was obvious they had to be killed quickly, lest the good people take matters into their own hands and torch the Tolbooth.

'Normally such criminals would face trial—but these crimes were so great and involved so many, it was impossible to conceive a public trial of such fiends. Some wondered if the women would be spared, and whether the men would claim responsibility for their heinous deeds. The King declared them to be enemies of mankind. There was not to be a trial, no chance for Sawney to poison a jury with his black words. Their executions were to be swift, and the entire matter put to rest once and for all.'

'The next day he marched them down to the sands at Leith, and Sawney and the men were staked there. His majesty had experience with such matters, having bled many a witch in his time. The men had their privy parts cut off and tossed into the fires in front of them. Then they cut off their hands and tossed them into the fire. Finally, their feet were cut from them. From what my Pa told me, the men were half-awake as they saw their limbs burned. My Pa said that Sawney never flinched, never cried for mercy, but only bellowed curses at those who watched. They bled there on the sands of Leith. Finally, their infernal remains were torched, charred to nothing.'

'The women-folk repented didn't they?'

He shook his head. 'Nay ... they were defiant harpies until the end. They cursed words that are still unrepeatable today to those of us there watching them. There was hope that some of the women would try and spare themselves, but they couldn't—it was against their very nature.'

'What did they do to them?' Alister asked with hesitation.

'They set up three big stakes and tied the women and children to these. Priests were brought in to offer repentance, but none was taken. Fires were set, as though they were unholy witches. The flames consumed them. Their screams filled the air and echoed as far back as Edinburgh, or so it was said.'

The colour drained from Alister's face as Angus spoke. 'Even the children?' he asked in a soft voice, just above a whisper.

The older man nodded. 'All but one, or so the story goes.'

'One was spared?'

'A girl, the youngest of the Beans—barely able to walk. They would have bound her up with the others but for one of the men, a man from Girvan named Alec McDouglas. My Pa heard him plead with the king that such a young girl, so innocent, could not have taken part in the crime of her parents, and ask that she be spared. Apparently the King consented, though nothing was said of this at the time. If any knew her true bloodline, they would seek revenge against her. Those that knew were sworn to secrecy. McDouglas and his wife could have no children, and Lillie, as he called her, was a blessing to them.

'So one was spared?' There was a glimmer of hope in the boy's eyes.

Angus licked his lips for a moment. *Do I dare tell him the rest of the tale?*

His wife spoke from the dry sink. 'What are you telling that boy Angus?'

'Nothing m'love, just a good ghost story,' he called back. He looked back at his grandson, and the boy understood that this was a secret bond between them.

Angus leaned forward so that his voice would not carry back to his wife. 'None of us knew about Lillie or her secret at the time. The men from Girvan that had accompanied the king to Edinburgh swore to keep it from the rest of the community. The hope was that she would redeem her upbringing and bloodline. And for a while, that was the case. Lillie grew up outside of town, and with the love of the McDouglases, blossomed into a pretty lass. Then ... then things changed.'

'What happened to her?'

'None of us know for sure. Some say that someone told her about her true parents. Others have said that her blood finally showed. As she grew older, her mind went. Most women married, but she wanted nothing to do with anyone outside of her parents. Then came that plague just before you were born. Her parents were taken from her by the fever, and with them went the last of her mind.

'It was just after you were born. Someone spoke up at church about her—one of the men who discarded his oath of silence. He broke faith and told the parishioners that she was a Bean; that there were many families who had lost loved ones to them; and how this half-crazed woman living in alone in their town. Well, it was too much for them. The Bean blood was something that could not be spared, even after all of these years. The wounds that some carried were far too deep.'

'What did they do to her?' whispered Alister, so his grandmother could not hear.

'Mobs are a strange thing laddie. They wanted to burn her like the others, at least that was what I heard—let her share the same fate as her accursed family. But someone pointed out that she had planted a hairy tree in front of her house as a child, though honestly that tree was there before she was born, from what I remember. Someone said they should hang her from her own tree, right there at the edge of Girvan. Rope was found and Lillie was bound and strung up. They told her why they were killing her, and that she was the product of incest most foul. She pleaded for mercy, and denied that it could be true. But the men my age, and a few older, remembered that one child had been spared by McDouglas. The crowd didn't want her living in the community, didn't want a Bean left alive wandering the countryside. You canna blame them for that Alister. Their crimes were so great that leaving a drop of Bean blood alive was something that could not be risked. Despite her pleas and cries, the rope was pulled taut. She hung from that hairy tree for three days, swinging in the westerly winds. Her body was cut down and buried in an unmarked grave.'

'Oh …'

'That tree died the next year of some sort of root rot, others say she had cursed it. They cut it down. No one spoke of it. But they say, when the winds of autumn kick in, you can hear Lillie's body swaying in the bows where that tree once stood.' He paused and let the story sink in.

'So then lad, when your gran' ma tells you to eat your greens or Sawney Bean will get you, she means it. Now then, you get back in there and finish your dinner.'

The boy nodded nervously, then sprang to the kitchen. Angus leaned back into his chair and pulled his blanket up tighter around his chest. Outside the winds of autumn were blowing hard.

2

The Origins of the Legend

> Cannibalism is rarely mentioned in archaeology textbooks. But there is clear evidence for cannibalism in almost every society and every period.[1]

Attempting to reach the root of the Bean folklore is tricky at best. Records from the period when the crimes allegedly took place do exist, but they are riddled with gaps. In addition, the story may have very well been passed by word of mouth from generation to generation for many years. The Bean saga may equally have been the creation of a fertile imagination in the sixteenth century. Thus, an exploration of the Beans' origins is required.

There is circumstantial evidence to suggest that the Bean folklore is deeply rooted in the history of the Galloway region, namely references to specific locales and inhabitants. Therefore, the most basic understanding of the history of Galloway and its people may help to comprehend the legend. This chapter will deal with the historical perspectives of Galloway and the people who live there, and potential links to cannibalism in England and Scotland which may have served as the basis for the Beans.

Galloway

Sawney Bean, legend has it, was born eight miles away from Edinburgh, but lived in the Galloway region. The Beans allegedly operated in both Galloway and Ayrshire, but the legend only mentions Galloway because it has included parts of what is now Ayrshire over the centuries. Regardless of its designation, the area in question was the buffer zone between England and Scotland—ground contested by both kingdoms throughout history.

Galloway's boundaries abut near Ayrshire in the north, and Dumfriesshire in the east. Her southern boundaries are the shorelines of the Solway Firth and the Irish Sea, which marks her western edge. Galloway is just over sixty-three miles long and forty-three miles wide; its landscape is mountainous and undulating in the north, and a twisting coastline in the south. The unsettled weather of the region makes agriculture challenging, and the rearing of livestock has proven the best use for the land.

Prehistoric south-western Scotland was dominated by families who eked out a rough living along the coasts and among the rolling crags. People are believed to have first settled in the area around 9000 BC. Various tribes of Picts, Scots and Angles struggled to make a living in the region, and the first defensive hill forts in the region were constructed around 800 BC. The Romans gave the region its first documented name on one of their military expeditions, the 'Rhinns of Galloway.' They also described two tribes occupying this territory: the Selgove—also known as 'The Hunters'—and the Novante.[2] The origins of these peoples have been subject to debate, but it is believed they had Irish as well as prevalently Pict ancestry.

The Romans occupied the region for a relatively short period—beginning when Hadrian became emperor in AD 117—but were still responsible for establishing a series of forts and clearing the landscape in Galloway. Where now there are rolling green grass hills, in the time of the Romans there was once a dense forest of oaks and firs.[3]

With the Romans came Christianity: in AD 395, Pope Sircius consecrated Ninian as Bishop and gave him the mission of converting the Picts of Galloway to the teachings of the Church.[4] Ninian would become the first saint of the eighth century. While Christianity faced stern resistance from the locals in other parts of Britain and Scotland, Ninian was dramatically successful in converting the Picts.

In AD 409, Honorius freed the British provinces from the Romans, and in so doing created a cultural and political vacuum in the land. The vacuum was filled with a number of other tribes—the Atecott Picts, Annadale, Nithsdale, Strathclyde, Cymri, and Welsh—as well as some influences from the neighbouring Irish.[5] The Saxons then invaded Galloway, followed by the Vikings *c.* 796. Their legacy was supposedly to impart a piratical form of life on the local inhabitants, namely, a fierce sense of independence and high estimation of family/clan roots. Marauding became a way of life for those that lived along the coast. In 1057, Malcolm Ceannmor succeeded the throne of Scotia—which encompassed Galloway—and was successful in driving out the Norsemen, though it is believed that a significant number of them did remain in the region.[6]

Galloway was most likely dominated by the Brythonic region until the late seventh century, when it was formally ruled by the kingdom of Bernicia of England, and the influence of the Brittons brought a new wave of immigrants to the region. The occupants of the region, however, hoped to stand apart from either Scotland or England, and over the years various attempts were made to establish Galloway's independence. Jacob, Lord of Galloway, made one of the first recorded references to Galloway as an independently governed entity in 973.[7] When Scottish King David I invaded Northumberland, a significant portion of his military force came from Galloway. His invasion culminated in the Battle of the Standard in 1138, in which the men of Galloway demonstrated their boldness.

> And the column of Galwegians after their custom gave vent thrice to yell of horrid sound, and attacked the southern in such an onslaught that they compelled the first spearmen to forsake their post; but they were driven off again by the strength of the Knights and [the spearmen] recovered their courage and strength against the foe. And when the frailty of the Scottish lances was mocked by the denseness of the iron and wood, they drew their swords and attempted to contend at close quarters. But the southern flies swarmed forth from the caves with their quivers, and flew like closet rain; and irksomely attacked the opponents' breasts, faces, and eyes, [and] very greatly impeded their attack. Like a hedgehog with its quills so would you see a Galwegian bristling all around with arrows, and none the less brandishing his sword and its blind madness rushing forward now smite a foe, now lash the air with useless strokes.[8]

It was in this struggle that the men from the border region earned the title, 'The Wild Men of Galloway'.

The Battle of the Standard changed the perception of Galloway in the minds of both the Scottish and English. One of the men that led the Galloway forces in the battle, Fergus (a man believed to of Norse blood), was appointed the first Earl of Galloway for his service in the fight.

Being poised at the Southern edge of Scotland made Galloway a traditional site for any English incursions to the north. As one Scottish historian put it, 'It's definitely Scotland, but 500 years ago, this area was called the Debatable Lands, because no one knew if it belonged to England or Scotland'.[9] Over the centuries, the Scottish have suggested that the loyalties of the people of Galloway leant towards the English, and there is evidence to support this. At the same time, the English have always viewed Galloway as part of Scotland. In the middle stood a people who were in fact doggedly independent.

Fergus's sons Uchtred and Gilbert accompanied King William the Lion of Scotland on his ill-fated expedition into England in 1173. The men of Galloway who marched off to battle were daring and courageous.

> They were fleet, naked, remarkably bold, wearing on their left sides small knives, formidable to any armed man, very expert in throwing and aiming their javelins at great distances, setting up for a signal when they [went] to battle a long lance.[10]

King William was captured in a reckless charge at the Battle of Alnwick. He led his men into the fight yelling, 'Now we shall see which of us are good knights!'[11]

English King Henry II's response to this was to send an English Army north, through Galloway, into Scotland. In order to free himself and those captured, William accepted the Church of England's dominion over the Scottish Church. William was forced to subjugate himself to Henry II, and pay a massive ransom—the costs of the English Army's occupation of Scotland—which he paid by inflicting enormous taxes on his people. This submission, sealed with the signing of the Treaty of Falaise, was met with uproar in Galloway. When Uchtred and Gilbert returned home,

> they drove out of Galloway all the independents and magistrates put over them by the Scotch King, they slew all the English and French who fell into their hands, took and destroyed all the castles and fortresses that the King of Scotland had built in their country, putting to the sword all they found in them.[12]

The people of Galloway vented their anger at the Treaty of Falaise at both parties—the King of Scotland and the King of England. This series of actions were destined to have dire consequences.

King Henry II was far from passive, and upon the advice of King William, sent an army into Galloway to quell the uprising. The two brothers, Uchtred and Gilbert, struggled with where their loyalties lay outside of Galloway proper. Uchtred leaned towards support of Scotland, whereas Gilbert was supported English rule. Their split mirrored the internal struggle that Galloway faced given its geographic location. Gilbert quickly submitted to English domination, and—aided by the English—arrested his brother, whom he had cruelly put to death at Loch Fergus. He took his nephew Roland, the son of Uchtred, as a hostage.[13] Henry II's army squashed Galloway's dreams of independence, and Gilbert turned over hostages of those families that had risen up for its independence. After his uncle's death, Roland went on to rule the part of Galloway called Carrick and, over the course of years, restored his rule over all of Galloway.

As a result of these power struggles, the Galwegians became accustomed to conflict, and in fact often sought it out among themselves.

> They raided, at first, to survive; it later became a way of life. These were the border raiders; the independent, lawless clans who cared nothing for authority, save that of family and chief. According to reports, they were 'a perverse and crooked people'. They were certainly condemned by the governments of both lands. Yet, in a perverse way, it suited the

powers that were to have these wild men guarding the edges of their kingdoms.[14]

Galloway became known to outsiders for the horses that were bred there; Galloway ponies, now extinct, were known for their short stature and rugged strength. William Shakespeare referred to them as 'Galloway nags' in the second part of *Henry IV*.[15]

Despite its turmoil, Galloway was integral to the history of the Scottish people. William Wallace tramped the grounds of Galloway fighting for Scottish freedom, pursuing a small English force through the Nith valley in Dumfriesshire. When the English attempted to seek refuge in Dumfries Castle, they found the gates closed and barred to them. Wallace rallied the region, eventually catching the English at Cockpool on the Solway Coast, and defeating them.

The people of the Galloway region were viewed as barbaric, and struggled with the desire to carve out a piece of Scotland that was their own. In 1236, a group of nobles once more attempted to establish Galloway's independence—the final such bid in her history.

> ... the powerful men from the various provinces of the West, namely from Galloway, the Isle of Man, and parts of Ireland, assembled at the instance of Hugh de Lacy, whose daughter had been married to Alan of Galloway, lately deceased, and they all united together for the purpose of restoring Galloway to the illegitimate son of the aforesaid Alan, and the annulling by force of the just disposition made by the king of Scots, who had distributed the inheritance amongst the three daughters of Alan, to whom it belonged by hereditary right.
>
> In order, therefore, to revoke and annul his distribution and restore the territory to the aforesaid Thomas, or to the son of Thomas, Alan's brother, or at least to one of that family, these presumptuous chiefs flew to arms, and, bursting forth into insolence, endeavoured to free themselves from the authority of the king. [...] they entered into a strange kind of treaty, by means of a certain mode of divination, yet according to the abominable custom of their ancestors. For all these barbarians and their chiefs and magistrates drew blood from a vein near the heart, and poured it into a large cup, they then stirred and mixed it up, and afterwards, drinking to one another, quaffed it off, as a token that they were from that time forth allied by an indissoluble and [...] kindred treaty, and indivisible both in prosperity and adversity, even at the risk of their heads.
>
> They therefore provoked the king and the kingdom to war, burning their own houses and those of their neighbours, that the king, when

he arrived, might not find either shelter or food for his army, and indulged in rapine and incendiarism, heaping injury on injury. On hearing of this, the king of Scotland collected his forces from all quarters, and [...] engaged the men in open battle; and the fortune of war turning against the Galwegians, they were put to flight, and the royal troops, pursuing them at the sword's point, slew many thousands of them, and those that were taken alive by the king and his soldiers were put to an ignominious death without any chance of ransoming themselves.[16]

Thus expired the thoughts and hopes of an independent Galloway.

Yet Galloway's role in Scottish history was far from over. Robert the Bruce passed through the region too. In Dumfries in 1306, he confronted John Comyn, a rival for the Scottish crown at the Greyfriar's Monastery. Comyn had allegedly betrayed Robert, and when faced with the charges, the two men came to blows, in which Comyn was mortally wounded on the high altar of the church.

Those clans that settled in the region held much of Scotland in their sway. The Douglases—who have played a vital role in Scottish history—were based in Galloway, at magnificent Drumlanrig castle; and the Maxwells lived on the Solway at Caerlaverock Castle.

Clan rivalries were not uncommon: Galloway clans such as the Bells, Armstrongs, Moffats, Crichtons, Maxwells, Irvings, and Johnstones often took up arms against each other or found themselves on opposing of the battle field. The Maxwells and Johnstones became locked in a feud that dragged on for years, culminating in the Battle of Dryfe Sands in Lockerbie in 1593. The bloodlust between the families was so great that eleven-year-old boys were armed and put into the saddle to fight. The powerful Maxwells were nearly wiped out as a result of feuding, giving rise to the expression 'Lockerbie Lick,' to describe an almost complete victory over a foe.

Such was the way of life in the thirteenth to sixteenth centuries, that when a baby boy was christened, his right hand was kept out of the ceremonial bath, 'all the better that he could strike unhallowed blows on the enemy'.[17] As more than one Scottish historian has pointed out, while the Highlanders in the North fought themselves, the lowlanders and peoples of Galloway were left to hold the line against the English.[18]

Mary Queen of Scots was no stranger to the region, though her final visit was far from illustrious. After her forced abdication of the throne, and the loss of the Battle of Langside, Mary fled south through Galloway, crossing the Solway of Firth in a fishing boat on 16 May 1568.

Galloway is described by the historian Buchannan as

possessing an undulating surface, and containing in the valleys between the hills almost innumerable lakes and fens, which, being now drained, form beautiful fields of rich and well-cultivated land.[19]

In the nineteenth century, Malcolm MacLachlan's regional study echoes Tytler's *History of Scotland*:

> The greater part of its whole extent was originally covered with natural wood, principally oak; and even hung tracts, now presenting nothing but barren and desolate moors and mosses, were then clothed with noble forests of oak, ash, beech, and other hard timber.[20]

Author Henry Inglis sums up his description of Galloway thus:

> there is no district of Scotland less generally known or worth knowing. Whether by sea or shore, from Maxwelltown to the Southerness, from Southerness to Carsluith, from Carsluith to Loch Moan, from Loch Moan to Maxwelltown, again south or west, or north or east, there is no district of Scotland more rich in romantic scenery and association, few of which possess the same combination of sterile grandeur and Arcadian beauty, and fewer still which are blessed with a climate equal in mildness of temperature to that of Galloway.[21]

So how did such a land of magnificent beauty and contrast, a land embroiled in fighting for centuries, foster such a legend as that of Sawney Bean and his family? The secret may lie in the traditional stories and history of cannibals in Scotland and England.

Cannibalism

Instances of cannibalism are far from rare in human history. In central Europe, legends of cannibals between the Dnieper and the Don rivers abound. Mongolia, China, Bulgaria, and Russia all have oral histories of cannibalism.[22]

> Claims of cannibalism among Neanderthals (notably at Krapina in Croatia) and modern humans have also been advanced. Perhaps the most compelling evidence comes from the transitional Mesolithic-Neolithic site at Fontbr'goua Cave in south-eastern France, excavated by Paola Villa, where cut-marked human and deer bones occur in the same assemblages, apparently butchered in closely analogous ways.[23]

Cannibal tribes have been discovered in the Pacific and in the Amazon as recently as in the twentieth century, one tribe being found in the late 1950s. Each new story to emerge about human beings eating each other stirs both fear and imagination.

The consumption of human flesh is a taboo that dates back to antiquity. In Greek mythology, Tantalus provided a feast for the gods, prepared with the flesh of his own son, Pelops. All of the gods detected the deception, with the exception of Demeter, who consumed a piece of his shoulder; the gods then restored Pelops to life, though he was missing a shoulder, and banished Tantalus to Tartarus (the part of the Underworld reserved for those who had deliberately committed evil).

Actual cannibalism is not unheard of in the British Islands. In 1903, the earliest human remains were found in the Gough Cave (also known as the Cheddar Gorge) near Somerset. The skeletal remains of a complete man who lived 14,700 years ago—dubbed the 'Cheddar Man'—were recovered, and have remained the centre of archaeological interest ever since the initial discovery. By 2001, a more detailed analysis of the recovered 'Cheddar Man' remains suggested that cannibalism had taken place. 'These people were processing the flesh of humans with exactly the same expertise that they used to process the flesh of animals,' said Professor Chris Stringer of the Natural History Museum in London, 'they stripped every bit of food they could get from those bones'.[24] The techniques used by the humans living in the cave indicated that they possessed 'sophisticated butchering techniques to strip flesh from the bones of men, women, and children'.[25] Evidence of prehistoric cannibalism was overwhelming: one recovered human femur had been split the length of the book so that the bone marrow could be scraped out for consumption. There were signs that humans had been murdered in the cave, their skulls crushed in. Whether they were killed purely for the purpose of consumption is unclear.[26]

The inhabitants of the cave did not just eat the dead people, but turned their remains into utensils. 'If you look around the world there are examples of skull-cups in more recent times—in Tibetan culture, in Fiji in Oceania, and in India,' said Dr Silvia Bello, a palaeontologist and lead author of a paper on the subject in the *PLoS One* journal. 'So, skulls have been used as drinking bowls, and because of the similarity of the Gough's Cave skulls to these other examples, we imagine that that's what these ancient people were using them for also'.[27]

Scottish Cannibals

Galloway, Sawney Bean's place of origin, has a long-standing tradition of cannibalistic behaviour, dating back to the Roman era.

The Attacotti are first mentioned in Roman records in the fourth century, according to which they inhabited the south-western region of modern-day Scotland. Their exact origins are unknown, but there is evidence that they may have come from Ireland. The Romans depict them as marauding mobs, and at least one reference to them inferred cannibalistic tendencies. When the Attacotti were serving the Romans as auxiliaries in Gaul, they were reputed to 'cut off and eat portions of men and women as dainties in preference to the sheep and oxen which they could have had'.[28]

It is unlikely that any of these early accounts of cannibalism directly formed the basis of the tale of Sawney Bean. They do establish that the practice of eating other human beings was not entirely uncommon, but the method of transference of such stories remains uncertain, especially given the mobility of the peoples of Galloway.

For tales of cannibalism with more potential relevance to Sawney Bean, one must look at more recent (recorded) history. In *History of Civilisation*, nineteenth-century historian Henry Buckle deals with the condition of Scotland at the end of the fourteenth century. He observes:

> There were cannibals in the land; and we have it on contemporary authority that a man and his wife who were at length brought to justice, subsisted during a considerable period on the bodies of children, whom they caught alive in trips, devouring their flesh and drinking their blood.[29]

Another such incident took place in Perth in 1339. At the time, the region was lousy with famine. A young and spoiled man named Crysticleik, together with his wife, allegedly survived off of the flesh of humans and drank their blood. He was known to lay traps for them, strangulate his victims, and devour them 'as wolves, lived out their flesh'.[30]

Historian Raphael Holinshed records another instance of cannibalistic behaviour eerily similar to the legend of the Bean family's activities.

> In the same year [1341, as some do write] or [according to others] in the year following there was such a miserable dearth, both through England and Scotland, that the people were driven to eat the flesh of horses, dogs, cats, and such like unused kinds of meats, to sustain their languishing lives withal, yea, insomuch that [...] there was a Scottishman, an uplandish fellow named Tristicloke, spared not to steale children, and to kill women, on whose flesh he fed, as if he had been a wolf.[31]

Holinshed documented another case of cannibalism which eerily foreshadowed the Beans.

> There was a certain thiefe that with his family lived apart from the companie of men, remaining secretlie within a den in Angus [Forfarshire], called Fenisden, who used to kill young persons and feid on their flesh.[32]

Another historian, Robert Lindsay of Pitscottie, documented this case as well. 'This mischievous man' lived in 'Angus callit Fiendes den,' with his wife and family, and went after young children to satisfy his hunger: 'And the mair zoung [young] thai war, he held them the more tender and greater delecat'. When finally apprehended for his crimes, he and his family were all 'burnt,' excepting 'ane zoung lase of ane zeir auld, quhilk was sawit [saved] and brocht to Dundie, quhair she was fosterit and brocht upe'. The young girl was spared only for a short period of time, and at the age of nine was burned alive, 'for the samin cryme her father and mother was convict of'. The spectators cursed and scolded her for her 'dampnabill deidis[damnable deeds]'. Rather than be repentant in her last moments of life, the girl screamed back at those who were watching her burn: 'Gif me credit and trow me, gif zen had experience of either woman and mans flesche, ze wald think the same sa delicious that ze wald never forbear it againe'.[33]

Hector Boetius gives a similar account—maybe even variation—in the same period. He tells the story of a Scotch brigand and his wife and children, who were condemned to death when it was proved that they killed and ate their prisoners. The extreme youth of one of the girls excused her from capital punishment, but at twelve years of age, she was found guilty of the same crime as her father, and suffered capital punishment. This child had been well brought up, yet was purported to have developed her parents' appetite.[34]

These tales closely mirror the framework of the Sawney Bean legend. The cannibal man at their centre often lived with his wife and children in total isolation—removed from 'normal' society—and the family burned at their capture. The children of these murderers partook in the crimes; indeed, the girl raised in Dundee is reported to have taunted her killers that they would understand her desire for human flesh were they to taste it.

Folklore also contributed to the Bean saga, for instance, that surrounding a Perth butcher named Andrew Christie. During a well-documented period of famine in Scotland in around 1340, the butcher joined a group of scavengers and robbers in the foothills of the Grampians, and when one of the scavengers died, Christie plied his trade using the corpse to provide food for his companions. The band of highwaymen developed a taste for human flesh, and with Mr. Christie as their leader, increased their ambushes of travellers, killing and eating horses and their owners alike. In a typical attack, Christie would spring from a bush and pull his victims off their mounts with a 'cleke,' commonly known as a crook or meat hook. Christie and his men supposedly killed thirty riders, and eventually caught the attention of the authorities in Perth, who sent an armed party to apprehend the killers. Christie managed to evade them, and returned to society under a new name. The bit of folklore was a common tale in Scotland at the time, and features in Andrew Cheviot's *Proverbs, Proverbial Expressions And Popular Rhymes Of Scotland*:

> They resorted to cannibalism at the instigation of their leader, Andrew Christie, a Perth butcher. This monster lay in wait for passing horsemen, and dragged them from the saddle with a large iron hook fixed to a long pole, hence his nickname. It is said Christiecleek died many years after, a married man and prosperous merchant in Dumfries. For centuries the mere mention of the word Christiecleek was sufficient to silence the noisiest child. [35]

But this tale does not bear up to historical scrutiny—it lacks evidence to support it beyond the realm of local legend. At the same time the parallels between Andrew Christie and Sawney Bean cannot be ignored. We have a band of robbers who consume their victims, and an armed party sent to apprehend them. The difference in the tale of 'Christiecleek' is that the butcher manages to escape and re-join civilisation, and that it was not put to print. In its transmission to the written page, Sawney Bean accrued an air of legitimacy that opened it up to further interpretation.

The Printed Tale

Scholars of Sawney Bean have, historically, had a chicken-and-egg debate about the first printed version of the legend. Authors such as William Roughead (*Rogues Walk Here*) and Ronald Holmes (*The Legend of Sawney Bean*) maintain that the first print rendition of the Bean tale appeared in chapbooks before it did in 'book' form. The problem—which both men acknowledge—is that there is no evidence to support this theory.

These chapbooks were pamphlets of the late seventeenth and early eighteenth century, printed in an octavo format (a sheet of paper folded in eight and making a book of sixteen pages). Later versions in the 1800s were also printed, in twelve- and twenty-four-page formats, and the paper they were printed on was of inexpensive newspaper stock.[36]

Another form of chapbook common to England in the 1800s was known as the broadsides, or broadsheets—printed on large sheets of paper, and, uncut, closely resembling modern-day broadsheets. These were sometimes sold as a single sheet—or more commonly cut down to form a booklet of eight to twelve pages—and favoured the printing of popular ballads, poems, and contemporary 'true crimes' Sawney Bean's. The two forms of printing are so similar that the distinctions are not really necessary. They were the sensational press of the time—the line between fact and fiction was commonly blurred for the sake of entertainment and commerce.

> [Chapbooks] are the relics of a happily past age, one which can never return, and we, in this our day of cheap, plentiful, and good literature, can hardly conceive a time when in the major part of this country, and to the larger portion of its population, these little Chap-books were nearly the only mental pabulum offered.[37]

None of these chapbooks or broadsides contained any real news. They speculated on a wide spectrum of phenomena, from war and intrigue abroad, local horror stories, and 'true crimes,' to short poems and documented ballads. The tales were short, often dramatic, and deliberately provocative. These were the tabloid papers of the era.

They were called chapbooks because they were sold by a Chapman, a form of peddler common to England and Europe in the nineteenth century. Chapmen led a difficult life, carrying their trinkets and wares in a wooden box strapped around the neck, and peddling them to passers-by. They were also referred to as 'flying' or 'running' stationers, and were usually accredited a dishonest reputation: 'Hawkers, Vendors, Pedlars, petty Chapmen, and *unruly* people'.[38] In *Love's Labour Lost*, 'Beauty is bought by judgment of the eye, Not uttered by base sale of Chapmen's tongues,' Shakespeare chimes in.[39]

The chapbooks were sold for a penny, and sometimes as part of a series. They were passed around, and not many were preserved on account of the poor quality of the paper. Their content was accessible to all, and their inexpensive cost made them available to anyone who could read—in contrast to the books sold by merchants. And finally, chapbooks gave the everyman a taste of tantalizing stories, whether they were real or not.

Several of these chapbooks, which will be presented in the following chapter in detail, tell the story of Sawney Bean. The collection in the National Library of Scotland is duplicated in several other libraries, but can claim some of the best preserved chapbooks of the age, as seen in Appendix A.

In analysing these chapbooks, one can clarify the dates when these items were printed. The first one was printed by Jollie and Sons of Carlisle. Jollie was in the printing business, and published the *Carlisle Journal* in the 1770s; his sons took over the business in 1819. Another chapbook printed with the 'Jollie and Sons' trademark dates back to the nineteenth century.[40]

A chapman in John Ashton's *Chap-Books of the Eighteenth Century* (Piccadilly: Chatto and Windus, 1882).

The Aldermary Churchyard was a leading chapbook factory, and the proprietors of this printing house were William and Cluer Dicey, though in later years, only William ran the business. The Diceys' production facilities accounted for the vast majority of chapbooks printed in London, yielding over 120 titles. To further complicate matters, most of the chapbooks printed by this establishment all bear the date 1750, regardless of the actual year that they were printed.[41] Historians Sandy Hobbs and David Cornwell have extensively researched the publication of the Bean story and come to the conclusion that

> There is no firm evidence of their [the Diceys] being at Aldermary Churchyard before 1764, so a conservative judgment would be that the surviving chapbook dates from around that time.[42]

The two slightly different chapbooks printed by Ferraby, at Butchery, Hull, can be traced to the early nineteenth century, around the time that Ferraby moved from Butchery to Market Place in 1802 or 1803.[43]

The British Library maintains an extensive collection of chapbooks also relating to Sawney Bean, as listed in Appendix B.

The British collection of chapbooks dates from 1800 to 1839, near the end of the chapbook era. The Scottish Library collection dates from approximately 1764 to1802. It is conceivable that earlier editions of this story were printed in chapbook form, but there is thus far no evidence to suggest that chapbooks were the first manifestation of the legend in print.

So if not chapbooks, then what was the first printed edition of the Bean saga? That distinction falls to Captain Charles Johnson, the mysterious author of a book that we can presume formed the basis for the chapbook variants—*A General and True History of the Lives and Actions Of the Most Famous Highwaymen, Murderers, Street-Robbers, &c. To Which is Added, A Genuine Account of the Voyages and Plunders, Of the Most Noted Pirates. Interspersed with several remarkable Tryals Of the Most Notorious Malefactors ... at the Sessions-House in the Old Baily, London. Adorn'd with the Effigies, and Other Material Transactions of the Most Remarkable Offenders, Engraved on Copper Plates.*

Captain Charles Johnson's version of the Bean story first appeared in print in London in 1724, and was reprinted several times, including in Glasgow in 1734. Captain Charles Johnson's identity is unknown, but his title and his allusions to pirates seems to imply that he was a ship's captain. A Charles Johnson is known to have written a play in 1712 entitled *The Successful Pirate*, which may or may not be the same man.

Pundits argue that the absence of a chapbook does not disqualify the genre from being the potential source of material for Captain Charles Johnson's oeuvre, but further exploration is needed. This is a possibility which would explain why most of Johnson's stories conveniently fit within the chapbook format in terms of length. Several of the stories did appear in chapbooks in later years, but none could be found by this author prior to the initial publication of Johnson's tome. Another book from the period—*A Compleat History of the Lives and Robbers of the most Notorious Highway-men, Foot-pad, Shop-lifters, and Cheats of both sexes, in and about London and Westminster, and all parts of Great Britain, for above an Hundred Years past, continued to the present time. The fifth Edition (adorn'd with Cuts), by Captain Alexander Smith, London 1719*—was a compilation of chapbooks and popular broadsheets printed in the era. Oddly enough, the story of Sawney Bean and his family does not appear in this edition, while it does share some of the stories— slightly reworded—from Captain Johnson's edition; this implies that they may have had the same source, or that Smith was plagiarised in later renditions.

In 1934, the historian and scholar John Robert Moore produced a theory that Captain Charles Johnson was a pseudonym for the famed author Daniel Defoe, author of *Robinson Crusoe* and other pirate-related tales. It wasn't for another fifty years that other scholars (P. N. Furbank and W. R. Owe) rejected this theory, and argued that the stylistic differences between Defoe and Johnson's works far outweighed their similarities. The concept that the famous author Daniel Defoe may have been responsible for the tale of Sawney Bean is tantalizing, but lacks solid evidence.[44]

There is still nothing to disprove that the chapbook version of the story was not circulating at the time that Smith wrote, merely that it was not included. When we consider that these books were for the most part reprints of stories already published in chapbooks or broadsheets, it is a plausible theory that simply lacks tangible evidence. As such, we have to look at the Johnson work as the first 'literary' publication of the Bean tale. It contains the essence of the legend as it would be told today. The following is a transcript of that version.

THE following Account, though as well attested as any historical fact can be, is almost incredible, for the monsterous and unparallel'd Barbarities that it relates; there being nothing that we have ever heard of, with the same Degree of Certainty, that may be compar'd with it, or that shows how far a brutal Temper, untam'd by Education and Knowledge of the World, may carry a Man in such glaring and horrible Colours.

Sawney Beane was born in the County of East Lothian, about eight or nine Miles eastward of the City of Edinburgh, some Time in the Reign of Queen Elizabeth, whilst King James I. govern'd only in Scotland. His Parents worked at Hedging and Ditching for their Livelihood, and brought up their Son to the same Occupation. He got his daily Bread in his Youth by these Means; but being very much prone to Idleness, and not caring for being confined to any honest Employment, he left his Father and Mother, and ran away into the desart Part of the Country, taking with him a Woman as viciously inclin'd as himself. These two took up their Habitation in a Rock by the Sea-side, on the Shore of the County of Galway, where they lived upwards of 25 Years without going into any City, Town, or Village.

In this Time they had a great Number of Children and Grand-Children, whom they brought up after their own Manner, without any Notions of Humanity or Civil Society. They never kept any Company, but among themselves, and supported themselves wholly by robbing; being, moreover, so very cruel, that they never robb'd any one, whom they did not murder.

By this bloody Method, and their Living so retiredly from the World, they continued such a long time undiscovered, there being no body able to guess how the People were lost that went by the Place where they lived. As soon as they had robb'd and murder'd any Man, Woman, or

Child, they used to carry off the Carcas to the Den, where cutting it into Quarters, they would pickle the mangled Limbs, and afterwards eat it; this being their only Sustenance: And, notwithstanding, they were at last so numerous, they commonly had Superfluity of this their abominable Food; to that in the Night-time they frequently threw Legs, and Arms of the unhappy Wretches they had murdered, into the Sea, at a great Distance from their bloody Habitation. The Limbs were often cast up by the Tide in several Parts of the Country, to the Astonishment and Terror of all the Beholders, and others who heard of it. Persons who have gone about their lawful Occasions fell so often into their Hands, that it caused a general Out-cry in the Country round about, no Man knowing what was become of his Friend or Relation, if they were once seen by these merciless Cannibals.

All the People in the adjacent Parts were at last alarm'd, at such a common Loss of their Neighbours, and Acquaintances; for there was no travelling in Safety near the Den of these Wretches. This occasioned [their] sending frequent Spies into these Parts, many of whom never return'd again, and those who did, after died; [the] strictest Search and Enquiry could not find how these melancholy Matters happen'd. Several honest Travellers were taken up on Suspicion, and wrongfully hang'd upon bare Circumstances; several innocent Inn-keepers were executed for no other Reason than that Persons who had been thus loft, were known to have lain at their Houses, which occasion'd a Suspicion of their being murdered by them, and their Bodies privately buried in obscure Places, to prevent a Discovery. Thus an ill-placed Justice was executed with the greatest Severity imaginable, in order to prevent these frequent atrocious Deeds; so that not a few Inn-keepers, who lived on the Western Road of Scotland, left off their Business, for fear of being made Examples, and followed other Employments. This on the other Hand occasion'd many great Inconveniencies to Travellers, who were now in great Distress for Accommodation for themselves and their Horses, when they were disposed to bait, or put up for Lodging at Night. In a Word, the whole Country was almost depopulated.

Still the King's Subjects were missing as much as before: so that it was the Admiration of the whole Kingdom how such Villainies could be carried on, and not the Villains to be found out. A great many had been executed, and not one of them all made any Confession at the Gallows; but stood to it at the last, that they were perfectly innocent of the Crimes for which they suffer'd. When the Magistrates found all was in vain, they left off these rigorous Proceedings, and trusted wholly to Providence, for the bringing to Light the Authors of these unparallel'd Barbarities, when it should seem proper to the Divine Wisdom.

Sawney's Family was at last grown very large, and every Branch of it, as soon as able, assisted in perpetrating their wicked Deeds, which they still follow'd with Impunity. Sometimes they would attack four, five, or fix Footmen together, but never more than two if they were on Horseback. They were, moreover so careful, that not one Whom they fell upon should escape, that an Ambuscade was placed on every Side to secure them, let them fly which Way they would, provided it should never so happen that one or more got away from the first Assailants.

How was it possible they should be detected, when not one that saw them ever saw any Body else afterwards? The Place where they inhabited was quite solitary and lonesome; and when the Tide came up, the Water went for near two hundred Yards into their subterraneous Habitation, which reached almost a Mile under Ground; so that when some who had been sent arm'd to search all the By-Places about, have past by the Mouth of their Cave; they have never taken any Notice of it, not supposing that any Thing human would reside in such a Place of perpetual Horror and Darkness.

The Number of the People these Savages destroyed was never exactly known; but it was generally computed that in the twenty-five Years they continued their Butcheries, they had washed their Hands in the Blood of a thousand at least, Men, Women, and Children. The Manner how they were at last discover'd was as follows:

A Man and his Wife behind him on the same Horse, coming one Evening Home from a Fair, and falling into the Ambuscade of these merciless Wretches, they tell upon them in a most furious Manner. The Man, to save himself as well as he could, fought very bravely against them with Sword and Pistol, riding some of them down, by main Force of his Horse. In the Conflict the poor Woman fell from behind him, and was instantly murdered before her Husbands Face; for the Female Cannibals cut her Throat, and fell to sucking her Blood with as great a Gust, as if it had been Wine. This done, they ript up her Belly, and pulled out all her Entrails. Such a dreadful Spectacle made the Man make the more obstinate resistance, as [he] expected the same Fate, if he fell into their Hands. It pleased Providence, while he was engaged, that twenty or thirty from the same Fair came together in a Body; Upon which, Sawney Bean and his Blood-thirsty Clan withdrew, and made the best of their Way through a thick Wood to their Den.

This Man, who was the first that had ever fell in their Way, and came out' alive, told the whole Company what had happened, and showed them the horrid Spectacle of his Wife, whom the Murderers had dragg'd to some Distance, but had not Time to carry her entirely off. They were all struck with Stupefaction and Amazement at what he related, took him with them to Glasgow, and told the Affair to the Provost of that City, who immediately sent to the King concerning it.

In about three or four Days after, his Majesty himself in Person, with a Body of about four hundred Men, set out for the Place where this dismal Tragedy Was acted, in order to search all the Rocks and Thickets, that, if possible, they might apprehend this hellish Cure, which had been so long pernicious to all the Western Parts of the Kingdom.

The Man who had been attacked was the Guide, and care was taken to have a large Number of Bloodhounds with them, that no human Means might be wanting towards their putting an entire End to these Cruelties.

No Sign of any Habitation was to be found for a long Time, and even when they came to the Wretches Cave, they took no Notice of it, but were going to pursue their Search along the Sea-Shore, the Tide being then out. But some of the Blood-hounds luckily enter'd this Cimmerian Den, and instantly set up a most hideous Barking, Howling, and Yelping; so that the King, with his Attendants, came back, and looked into it. They could not yet tell how to conceive that any Thing human, could be concealed in a Place where they saw nothing but Darkness. Nevertheless, as the Blood-hounds encresed their Noise, they went farther in, and refused to come back again, they began to imagine there was some Reason more than ordinary. Torches were now immediately sent for, and a great many Men ventur'd in through the most intricate Turnings and Windings, till at last they arrived at that private Recess from all the World, which was the Habitation of these Monsters.

Now the whole Body, or as many of them as could, went in, and were all so shocked at what they beheld, that they were almost ready to sink into the Earth. Legs, Arms, Thighs, Hands, and Feet of Men, Women, and Children, were hung up in Rows, like dried Beef. A great many Limbs lay in Pickle, and a great Mass of Money, both Gold and Silver, with Watches, Rings, Swords, Pistols, and a large Quantity of Cloaths, both Linnen and Woollen, and an infinite Number of other Things, which they had taken from those whom they had murder'd, were thrown together in Heaps, or hung up against the Sides of the Den.

Sawney's Family at this Time, besides him, consisted of his Wife, eight Sons, six Daughters, eighteen Grandsons, and fourteen Grand-Daughters, who were all begotten in Incest. These were all seiz'd and pinion'd, by his Majesty's Order in the first Place; then they took what human Flesh they found, and buried it in the Sands, afterwards loading themselves with the Spoils which they found, they return'd to Edinburgh with their Prisoners, all the Country, as they passed along, flocking to fee this cursed Tribe. When they were come to their Journey's End, the Wretches were all committed to the Tolbooth, from whence they were die next Day conducted under a strong Guard to Leith where they were all executed without any Process, it being thought needless to try Creatures who were even professed Enemies to Mankind.

The Men had first their Privy-Members cut off, and thrown into the Fire before their Faces, then their Hands and Legs were severed from their Bodies; by which Amputations they bled to Death in some Hours. The Wife, Daughters, and Grand-Children, having been made Spectators of this just Punishment inflicted on the Men, were afterwards burnt to Death in three several Fires. They all in general died without the least Signs of Repentance; but continued cursing and venting the most dreadful Imprecations to the very last Gasp of Life.[45]

The salient elements, possibly taken from the existing stories of cannibalism in Scotland, are all in place in this version. Thus began the story of the Bean cannibals' renewal: from folklore into printed history, from this back into folklore, and finally into modern media.

3
The Legend's Sordid Past

> Lies are not worth a farthing if they are not calculated for the effectual deceiving of the people they are intended to deceive.[1]

Several authors and historians who have delved into the tale of Sawney Bean have gone as far as to insist that the story was printed as a form of English propaganda against the Scottish nation. According to Ronald Holmes, whose research into the Bean myth has set the standard since the 1970s,

> It is highly indicative that the legend of Sawney Bean was published only in England during the first hundred years of its existence in print. Since it combined a sense of wonder, degradation of a traditional enemy and so many well-known aspects of folk-tale and history it must have been something of a best seller.[2]

He further states:

> Accusations of cannibalism as a weapon of propaganda is very old indeed and was used during this period. It was used during the Great Rebellion in England and was to be used again against the French during the Revolution. Against this background it may be believed that the legend of Sawney Bean was used as anti-Scottish propaganda. If so, it seemed to have some success, for the evidence shows that some people believed that the Scots ate children during the 1745 Rebellion.[3]

Unfortunately, Holmes offers no evidence to support his claim.

Was the legend nothing more than a tale intended to degrade the people of Scotland? If so, was it a byproduct of the era, intertwined with the historical events surrounding it? This chapter will explore the events just prior to the first publication, and the grounds for considering this tale a piece of anti-Scottish propaganda.

The Covenanter Movement and Religious Rebellions in the Seventeenth Century

The story of the Beans was first printed in early 1700s and perpetuated mostly in the eighteenth century, around which time two important events occurred and would have been fresh in the minds of readers—the suppression of the Covenanters, and the Jacobite Rebellion of 1745.

The Covenanters were a Presbyterian movement primarily active in Scotland and involved in the signing of the National Covenant in 1638. The Scottish Presbyterians were centred in the lowlands of Scotland, especially in the Galloway region. The Covenanter Movement was came into being when the Stuart King Charles I introduced a Book of Common Prayer in Scotland (which is what prompted the National Covenant to be drawn up). King Charles stated that any opposition to the liturgy would be treated as treason, punishable by death.

The Stuarts kings strongly believed in the Divine Right of the monarchy. In their minds, God not only bestowed on them the right to lead the people they ruled, but also the spiritual leadership of the Church—in this case the Church of Scotland. Those who signed the Covenant of 1638 believed quite differently: it was their—and many Scots'— assertion, that only Jesus Christ could be their spiritual leader. Charles I was an Anglican, not a Presbyterian, and refused to hold a Presbyterian ceremony for his coronation, which was further interpreted as a threat to Scottish Presbyterians. The National Covenant itself was a mark of rebellion in the eyes of the king, for those who signed it were opposed to the Stuarts' spiritual claims over the Church, and regarded the Covenant as a contract between the people of Scotland and God in defiance of the king. Over 3,000 people signed the Covenant, and copies were printed and sent to every community in Scotland. Charles subsequently attempted to tighten the reins on Scottish Presbyterians, which prompted rioting, and then an outright rebellion.

The Covenanters raised an army of over 20,000 men against Charles I, and won several battles, including a significant victory at Marston Moor. Two years later, Charles sent his sons to Europe for safety, and eventually surrendered to the Scottish forces. He was urged to sign the Covenant and make peace, but he refused, at which point he was turned over to the English Parliament. Charles was able to rally the Scottish nobles who supported his return with the condition that he stop his oppression of Presbyterians. This split the Covenanter Movement: the nobles supporting him led an army to march into England, only to be defeated by Oliver Cromwell at Preston; and those who opposed the nobles, known as the 'Protestors', saw the defeat at Preston as God's Will that the king should not hold sway over the Church. They overthrew the remaining nobles in Edinburgh, and seized control of the government. With the Covenant Protesters' rise to power came reprisals against their opponents, namely floggings and executions. This was the apex of the Covenanter Movement.

In 1649, Cromwell's government tried and executed Charles I. Charles II returned to Scotland and signed the National Covenant so that he could safely assume the Scottish throne. The problem was that this was the era of parliamentary rule: Cromwell and his followers had no need for kings, and Charles II was a reminder of the past. In 1650, England invaded Scotland with the aim of toppling Charles II's reign: Cromwell's campaign was stalled and came close to total defeat, but the Covenanters chose this time to purge their ranks of those men who did not share their religious zeal. This purge did away with their most experienced soldiers and leaders, and the Covenanters were consequently utterly defeated at Dunbar. Young King Charles II fled to France, and the Covenanter Movement was shattered; Cromwell's forces occupied Scotland, and he became the Lord Protector of the realm.

After Cromwell's death, Charles II was proclaimed King of England in 1660. This was a strange period for Scotland: the Covenanters had almost completely fallen from power; the English Civil War had ended and so had Cromwell's regime; and there were now cries for complete democracy. Charles II responded to these new circumstances by both appointing his own bishops and demanding that ministers be supported by the local gentry and swear him an oath of allegiance. Galloway again became the focus of conflict, when over two-hundred ministers from that district would not meet Charles demands. Starting in New Luce, the rebellious ministers—the last fragment of the Covenanter Movement—began to preach, not in the kirks, but in barns, open fields, and wherever they could assemble followers. This was an act that defied Charles II's reforms, and its most vocal figure was the Reverend Alexander Peden of New Luce, Galloway.

Charles II entered into a treaty with King Louis XIV of France, in which he would bring Catholicism to Scotland in exchange for French support of England in the third Anglo-Dutch War. Peden and other Covenant leaders were captured, and the movement appeared for all intents and purposes crushed when—upon the Covenanter assassination of a bishop—Charles II sent a military force led by Viscount Dundee, John Graham of Claverhouse, into Scotland to suppress them. Claverhouse became known as one of the more vigorous hunters of Covenanter gatherings: he swept through southwestern Scotland and captured hundreds of them; those who resisted him were slaughtered.

At the Battle of Drumclog, Claverhouse's men attempted to arrest a large gathering of Covenanters, but, instead of mild-mannered church-goers, found them armed. Claverhouse pressed the attack but the group fought back viciously. Fighting on boggy ground and facing religious zealots, Claverhouse's militia were defeated, and he barely escaped with his life.[4] Glasgow fell to the Covenanters shortly thereafter, and once more the movement seemed poised for victory. The opportunity was ripe for the taking, for there was no military force in place to stop them.

However, the Covenanters could not unite under a single cause and got caught up in internal frictions. Their force settled in Bothwell Brig (bridge) south of Glasgow; they had hoped to organise themselves there, but found themselves arguing. Some opposed Charles II's rule because he had not respected the terms of the National Covenant he had signed, whereas others felt that they had a higher, religious obligation to topple the king, or declared that religious freedom was their true cause. Debate also raged in all of the factions as to whether those Scots who did not subscribe to the Covenant should be allowed to fight for the cause.

Internal bickering allowed the royal forces to reorganise and to attack them at their camp at Bothwell Brig on 22 June 1679: the English were victorious, and drove the survivors into flight across Galloway. Those who were captured were taken to the iconic Greyfriars' Kirkyard in Edinburgh, then more commonly known as the 'Covenanter's Prison', where the National Covenant had originally been signed.

The fate of Scotland was tightly bound with that of England and the royal lines of succession. Charles didn't have a legal heir, so his brother, James II, was confirmed as the successor to the realm. But James was openly Catholic in his beliefs, and this rekindled the fires of rebellion among Presbyterians. James II's Catholicism was further used as proof that the Stuarts were unfit to rule.

Matters were worsened when Claverhouse was once more sent into Galloway to root out opponents to Charles II's named successor, where he imposed an oath of loyalty ending with 'God Save the King'. Those who still supported the Covenanter Movement refused to utter such a phrase, and thus exposed themselves. A Highland army and troops loyal to the king were billeted in south-western Scotland to suppress any additional uprisings; Covenanter gatherings were arrested, and prisoners tortured and in some cases killed. This period was known as 'The Killing Time'.

James VII of Scotland and II of England assumed the throne upon the death of his brother Charles II in 1685. He infuriated those with Covenanter sympathies by appointing Catholics to positions of power, and faced two rebellions—one in England led by the Duke of Monmouth, and the other by Archibald Campbell, the Earl of Argyle in Scotland. While both were eventually suppressed, they shook the foundations of the monarchy.

When his son and legal heir James Francis Edward Stuart was born, the boy was raised Catholic, causing many to worry further about Rome's influence over the throne. Conspiracies began to hatch about toppling both James VII and II and his son. Indeed, the old rhyme that quips 'Rock a bye baby, on the tree top, when the wind blows, the cradle will rock [...]' refers to the precarious position of James II's son. The 'wind' alludes to William of Orange, James II/VII's son-in-law, and the 'cradle' to the House of Stuart.

Matters came to a head in 1688, when a loose alliance of English Parliamentarians supported by Scottish Covenanters encouraged the Protestant William of Orange—James VII and II's son-in-law— to invade England in the Glorious Revolution. William seized the throne, while James VII and II fled to France with his wife and heir. Though James VII and II never formally abdicated his position, his actions allowed William II of Scotland and III of England (or 'King Billy', as the Scots referred to him) to be recognised as ruler.

There were still die-hard supporters of the Stuart line—especially in Scotland. James clung to the notion that he might be able to return to power, if only in Scotland. While he fumbled with the Scottish parliament, but William II and III courted the nobles enough to sway their support in his favour.

Viscount Dundee, John Graham of Claverhouse—the great hunter and executioner of the Covenanters—still strongly supported James VII and II's claim to the throne, and he raised an army in the hope of winning back the Scottish throne for James. In May 1689, Claverhouse marched a small army from Lochaber to Blair Atholl; when the Williamite Army moved against him, Claverhouse caught the Williamites in the narrow gorge of Killiecrankie, and slammed into the king's men as they emerged from the pass. He defeated them at the Battle of Killiecrankie, but at the cost of his own life, for he was mortally wounded in the fighting. James VII and II himself was in Ireland fighting—and losing—the battles at Boyne in 1690 and 1691. His losses there caused him to retreat back to France in an attempt to regroup, which gave birth of the Jacobite movement—one which would cause damage to the Scottish image among the English in time for the legend of Sawney Bean's first publication.

William's rise to the throne brought the Covenanter Movement in Scotland full circle. The efforts of the Covenanters had contributed to the overthrow of the English crown, and had incited a half-century of civil war—all from its focal point in Galloway. These five decades of Anglo-Scottish tensions would reverberate for centuries, or at the very least planted the seeds for further rebellion less than a century later. Like any political upheaval, the Covenanter Movement would have unforeseen consequences—one of them was the Jacobite rebellion of 1745.

The Jacobite Rebellions

The term 'Jacobite' refers to a political movement with the sole aim of restoring the Stuart bloodline back to the Scottish and/or English throne. The self-exiled King James VII and II created a shadow government while in France, handing out positions and appointments as though he still were in power with the financial and political support King Louis XIV. He died on 6 September 1701, never living to see the restoration that he so dreamed of, and King Louis—who was at war with William II and III—immediately recognised his son, James VIII and III, as the rightful king of Scotland and England.

In a strange historical twist, the agent of change for the Scots came from a common ground mole. In 1702, William II and III's horse stumbled into a mole hole, toppling him and breaking the king's collarbone; pneumonia set in from the injury, and he died. The mole was toasted by the Jacobite supporters as 'the little gentleman in the black velvet waistcoat'.[5]

Succession to the throne was a complicated affair. William's wife Mary had died childless in 1694, eight years before William's demise. This left no direct successor to his bloodline, so Princess Anne became Queen of England on 8 March 1702. Anne's relation to the throne was complex: she was the daughter of James VII and II, and her sister Mary had been joint ruler with William II and III. After William's death, the throne went to the rotund Anne: she became the Queen of Scotland, England, and Ireland under the Acts of Union.

Anne had, at King Charles's insistence, been raised as a Protestant, which made her more appealing to the English and Scottish people. She had been pushed into marrying Prince George of Denmark by her father to off-set the power of his son-in-law William, who had usurped his throne. Anne, however, ruled with her own conscience.

After Anne's death in 1714, George II assumed the throne—the first of the Hanoverian kings. His coronation launched a political battle between the Tories and Whigs, which presented an opportunity for James VII and II's son, James Francis Edward Stuart, to assert his family's claim again. But rather than be so bold as to attempt to seize the whole of the British Isles, James set his eyes on Scotland alone.

To Scottish nobles, here was the chance to have a Scottish king for the first time since 1603. Seating the Pretender—James VIII and III was known as 'the Old Pretender' or 'the Old Chevalier'—on the Scottish throne would unburden them of English dominion. James VIII and III travelled with a French fleet destined for Scotland, where he hoped to be welcomed as their rightful ruler. Unfortunately, the fleet was intercepted and dogged by the English fleet, and the French Admiral refused to take James to shore for fear that he might be killed— the French king had ordered that they make no landing that might cost James his life. Eventually, James returned to France and began plans for a future expedition. Some historians estimate that 30 to 40,000 Scotsmen would have risen to his banner had he but set foot in Scotland, mostly out of their hatred of the concept of Union. Instead, the Cavalier Movement in the Scottish parliament took root—one of its founding tenets was *opposition* to any alliance with the House of Stuart.

When the long war with France and England concluded, one of the peace terms negotiated by the English was that the French monarchy would no longer provide political or financial support for James VIII and III. The Pretender found himself exiled to the Lorraine countryside in the Franco-German borderlands. While this appeared a low-point, his fortunes were about to change, for the next year brought James the uprising that he had hoped for.

The 1715 Jacobite uprising, known as 'the Fifteen', was launched when John Erskine, the Sixth Earl of Mar, joined several Highland chiefs and declared James VIII and III King of Scots. James set sail for Scotland, and finally landed on Scottish soil after the Battle of Sheriffmuir. He had been expecting a vast following, and was disappointed with the small rag-tag army that rallied to his cause. What was needed was a leader with charisma, one that would stir up the national fervour of all Scots, not just a few—but James VIII and III was not such a man. He was timid and uncomfortable with large crowds, and failed to capture the hearts of the Scottish people.

James fell ill during the winter, which further limited his ability to inspire the masses. Plans had been drawn up to have him crowned at Scone, the traditional seat of Scottish kings, but James squandered the opportunity for such an iconic gesture. Instead, he sailed back to France where, since the death of Louis XIV, he had become an embarrassment to the French government, and they wanted nothing to do him.

James VIII and III came to the slow and painful realisation that he might never regain the throne. In 1719, he married Maria Clementina Sobieska, the granddaughter of the Polish King. The Pope declared them King and Queen of England, which only seemed to cement resistance to him returning to the throne, out of fear that they attempt to re-enforce Catholicism. The Scottish and English were still mostly Protestant, and the Old Pretender's Catholicism hung like an albatross around his neck.

Clearly, any hope for the Stuart line lay within a future generation. On 31 December 1720, Charles Edward Stuart was born. He was raised to be the King of England, yet never set foot in England until 1745. While his father had been the Old Pretender, Charles was christened the Young Pretender, or 'Bonnie Prince Charlie' by the Jacobite Scots.

Bonnie Prince Charlie. His invasion of England helped sow the seeds for prejudice against the Scots.

Initially, there was little recompense in supporting the Young Pretender; neither did other European powers bolster his claim with troops and arms. This changed in 1743. France was embroiled in a war with Hanoverian Britain, and it was reaching a deadlock in the lowlands; the French saw Bonnie Prince Charlie as a means of opening a new front against the English. If he could be returned to England or Scotland, and mount a revolt there to press his claim for the throne, the English would be forced to respond, possibly reversing the war for the French.

If the French had had their way in the matter, the Jacobite Revolt of 1745—'the Forty-Five'—would have happened a year earlier. The Young Pretender stood ready for invasion of Scotland, but harsh weather conditions—seemingly a stalwart ally of Britain's—destroyed most of his fleet, so the invasion was stalled until 1745 while the French re-equipped the small invasion force.[6]

At the age of twenty-five, Charles landed on the west coast of Scotland at Eriskay on 23 July 1745. While the lowlands and Galloway region—still resistant to his claim in the aftermath of the Covenanter Movement—did not offer him an outpouring of support, the Highlanders overwhelmingly rallied to Bonnie Prince Charlie.

As his followers increased, the Young Pretender marched on Edinburgh and took the city on 16 September. Though Edinburgh castle overshadowed the city and was still held by the government, not a single shot was fired when Bonnie Prince Charlie seized the capital of Scotland and established himself in the Palace of Holyroodhouse (the traditional seat of the Scottish royal family).

The Young Pretender was daring, if nothing else. As more men assembled under his banners, he set his eyes towards the South. On 31 October, Charles set out to invade England—with his gaze set on London.

The invasion of England was stunningly fast, and almost unopposed. Panic gripped England: investors rushed into the Bank of England to withdraw their savings to the point of near-bankruptcy; Carlisle, Penrith, Preston, Manchester, Macclesfield, and Derby all fell into chaos in quick succession as the stock market collapsed; and rumours abounded that King George II was making preparations to flee London on the royal yacht.[7]

Bonnie Prince Charlie had expected the welcome of Jacobites in England, but only one regiment of supporters ever materialized; and the French had promised him troops to join his forces upon invasion, but these also never arrived. The English didn't flock to his aide, either: rather, rumour and propaganda had inculcated them with a deep fear of this Highland host.

> It is credibly affirmed that many of the women hid their children at their (the Scottish Army's) approach, under an impression that they were cannibals, fond, in particular, of the flesh of infants.[8]

The myth that the Scottish were inhumane consumers of other human beings spread without difficulty in England.

The Young Pretender held a council of war to determine whether his forces should march on London, which was his desire. A spy in the Scots' ranks had fed him information that a large English force had been sent to block his march—a complete fabrication—so Bonnie Prince Charlie's supporters grew nervous and voted to retreat back to Scotland. His army was only 130 miles away when it turned back from London, where—unknown to him—no credible force lay in wait. Had he marched on London, there would have been little to stop him from seizing the capital. Deception had saved the monarchy.

On 6 December 1745, the Jacobite Army started the march north. The day was named 'Black Friday' because it marked the highpoint of the Jacobite cause. The Army marched through Galloway, and spent a week there to rest and regroup; but the lowland Scots were not supportive of the Young Pretender, and eventually the Jacobites moved further north into the Highlander's mainstay. Besides, the retreat northwards had bought the English time to muster a force capable of pursuing the Jacobites and removing the Stuart threat once and for all. Led by the William Augustus, Duke of Cumberland and George II's younger and more favoured son, the English dogged the Jacobites and gave them little choice but to withdraw into the Highlands.

The two forces met on the fields of Culloden Moor the day after Bonnie Prince Charlie's birthday, 16 April 1746. The prince's forces had tried to ambush the English the previous evening, but had become lost in the heather and bogs and eventually stumbled back into camp, exhausted and hungry. When the armies met in battle on the 16th of April, it was an uneven contest at best. The Duke of Cumberland's forces were highly trained and regimented, disciplined in their fire, and supported by cannon fire. The Highlanders had a small supply of rifles and pistols, but primarily relied on a massed charge of swords and small shields ('targes') to overwhelm their enemies. It was the Highland charge, a style of combat that they believed would determine the course of battle.

Culloden was a disaster from the start. The grounds where they fought were poor: one flank of the battlefield was a muddy bog, which slowed the pace of the traditional Highlander tactics into a crawl. While the Jacobites had some artillery, they had to stand under withering musket fire on open ground, they had little command of the battlefield, and their leaders were ill-equipped in comparison to the English regulars. Bonnie Prince Charlie had his forces stand their ground in the hope of luring the English to advance, but the English pummelled their ranks with artillery fire. When the orders came through to attack, the Jacobites were not coordinated down the entire line; their left flank became mired in the windswept bog and heather, while the right flank punched through the English left, only to be engulfed in volley after volley of musket fire by the Duke of Cumberland's reserves. The Highlanders' charge had inflicted damage, but the bayonets of the English troops had done more.

In the end, the English lost 50 men, with 259 wounded, whereas the Jacobites had lost 1,500 to 2,000 men, with several hundred captured. The Jacobite Army melted and fled in full rout, with Bonnie Prince Charlie forced to flee the battlefield as well. It was the last major land battle on British soil.

The Young Pretender was forced to flee Scotland and return to France in shame and defeat.

What followed, dubbed 'the Pacification', changed Scotland forever: the English dismantled the clan system; the Highlands, hitherto a mysterious land where forces could take refuge, were mapped; and bagpipes were banned, labelled weapons of war. Scotland's identity was suppressed, even in the lowlands, where support of the Jacobites had been minimal.

Did This Turmoil Spawn Sawney Bean's Tale?

It was in this era that the legend of Sawney Bean and his cannibal host first appeared.

Was it possible that the story was the by-product of anti-Scottish propaganda on the part of the English? The Covenanter movement—which had started in the Galloway region—had already been responsible for toppling the English throne. Even if Captain Charles Johnson's first publication pre-dates 'the Forty-Five', 'the Fifteen' of the Jacobite movement were still in current memory.

From the English perspective, the rebellious Scottish people were once more fostering the overthrow of their King, which was bound to give birth to prejudice if it didn't exist already. Historians have accounted for the spread of the stories of Scottish cannibals prior to the 1745 uprising, and argued that it was indeed used to instil fear. So it is not hard to conceive that the stories were propaganda; but, short of an admission by the author, we have no way to verify with certainty that the tale of the Beans was part of a smear campaign.

What is in a name?

Additional support that the Bean folklore has its origins in England as a slight to the Scots is the use of the name 'Sawney' in the tale. Sawney was an English creation, short for the name Alexander, Alasdair, or Alistair—derived from the last two syllables. There is belief that the name 'Sawney' may have been a popular Scottish name from the south-west of Scotland, but the evidence is thin.

In the eighteenth century, rather than be tied to a shortening of Alexander, 'Sawney' became known as a slur defaming anyone of Scottish decent.

> In the days immediately after the accession of James VI. to the English throne, under the title of James I., to the time of George III. And the Bute Administration, when Scotsmen were exceedingly unpopular, and when Dr Samuel Johnson—the great Scoto-phobist, the son of a Scotch bookseller at Lichfield—thought it prudent to disguise his origin, and overdid his prudence by maligning his father's countrymen, it was customary to designate a Scotsman as a *Sawney*. The vulgar epithet, however is dying out, and is nearly obsolete.[9]

This was documented in 1888, and situates the beginnings of 'Sawney' as a smear-tactic as early as 1657.

This claim is substantiated by the popular period print, 'Sawney in the Bog House'—printed in 1779 by James Gillray—which depicted a man in a kilt and other Scottish garbs sitting on a communal toilet. This print, and variations of it, further instilled the derogatory implications of the name.

Prints such as 'Sawney in the Boghouse', which showed Scots as too stupid to use the lavatory, gave a distinctive eighteenth-century edge to traditional depictions of lice-ridden cannibalism. (Interestingly, the idea of Scots as cannibals, apocryphally realised in the legend of Sawney Bean, was also found in eighteenth-century English chapbook literature about the West Country: in such remote margins, what other kind of behaviour could be expected? This smear was of course exported to Africa in the colonial age.)[10]

Finally, there was the period expression, 'Sawney Ha'peth', or Sawney Half-Pence. This phrase was used to describe something that was worthless or fool. Its origins came from the union of Scotland and England in 1707, during which time a Scottish pound was worth one twelfth of a Sterling pound.

The slur seems to have endured over time in other trivia: the Official Scrabble Player's Dictionary lists 'sawney' as a word that means 'foolish'.[11]

Evaluating the Sawney Bean Chapbooks— the Aldermary Church Yard Edition

The earliest chapbook edition of the Bean saga known to exist came from the Aldermary Church Yard, roughly dated 1779 by the National Library of Scotland and definitely not printed prior to 1764. The following is a transcript of this version:

SAWNEY BEANE
AND
His FAMILY;
Robbers and Murderers

Who took up their Abode in a Cave, near the Sea-Side, where they lived
Twenty-five Years, without going once to visit any City, Town, or Village.
Computation, they Robbed and Murdered about one Thousand
Persons, whom they Eat; but at last were happily discovered by a Pack
of Blood-Hounds; when SAWNEY BEANE, his Wife, Eight Sons, Six

Daughters, Eight Grand-Sons, and Fourteen Grand-Daughters, were all seiz'd and Executed, in Manner hereafter specified.

Printed and Sold in Aldermary Church Yard, London

The
History
of
Sawney Beane

The following account, (tho' as well attested as any historical fact can be) is almost incredible; for the monstrous and unparalleled barbarities that it relates; there being nothing that we ever heard of with the same degree of certainty that may be compared with it, or that shows how far a brutal temper, untamed by education or knowledge of the world, may carry a man in such glaring and horrible colours.

Sawney Beane was born in the county of East Lothian, about eight or nine miles eastward of the city of Edinburgh, some time in the reign of Queen Elizabeth, whilst King James I. governed Scotland. His parents worked at hedging and ditching for their livelihood, and brought up their son in that occupation. He got his daily bread in his youth, by that means; but being very addicted to idleness and not choosing to be confined to any honest employment, he left his father and mother, and ran away to the desert part of the country taking with him a woman as viciously inclined as himself. These two took their habitation in a rock by the seaside on the shore of the county of Oalgay, where they lived upward of 25 years, without going into any city, town or village.

In this time they had a great number of children and grandchildren, whom they brought up after their own manner without the least notion of humanity or of civil society. They never kept any company but among themselves, and supported themselves by robbing; being moreover so very cruel that they never robbed any body whom they did not murder.

By this bloody method, and their living so retiredly from the world, they continued a long time undiscovered; there being no body able to guess how the people were lost, who went by the place where they lived. As soon as they robbed any one, they used to carry off their carcasses to their den, where cutting them in quarters they would pickle the mangled limbs, and afterwards eat them, these being their only subsistence.

The people in the adjacent parts were alarmed at so uncommon a loss of their neighbours; for there was no travelling safely near the den of those wretches: This occasioned spies in these parts, many of whom never returned again and those who did after the strictest search and enquiry, could not find out how these melancholy matters happened. There were several honest travellers, taken upon suspicion, and wrongfully hanged; several honest inn-keepers executed for no other reason that the persons who had been thus lost, were known to have lain at their houses; which occasioned a suspicion of their being murdered by them, and their bodies privately buried in obscure places, to prevent a discovery. Thus an ill-placed justice was executed with the greatest severity imaginable, to prevent their frequent atrocious deeds; so that not a few inn-keepers, who lived on the western road in Scotland left off their business, for fear of being made examples of, and followed other employments. This on the other hand, occasioned many inconveniencies to passengers who were now in great distress for want of accommodation for themselves and horses, when they were disposed to bait or to put up for lodging at night: In a word, the whole country was almost depopulated.

How then was it possible they should be detected, when not one that saw them ever perceived any body afterwards? The place they inhabited was solitary and lonesome, and when the tide came up, it went nearly two hundred yards into their cave, that which reached almost a mile under ground: so that when some have been sent armed, they have passed by the mouth of the cave without any notice; not supposing that a human creature could reside in such a place of horror.

The number of people they destroyed was never exactly known; but it was computed that in twenty-five years they had murdered at least one thousand men, women, and children. The manner they were at last discovered was as follows:

A man and his wife behind him on the same horse, coming one evening home from a fair, and falling into an ambuscade of these merciless wretches, they attacked them in a very furious manner. The man, to save himself, fought bravely riding some of them down by main force; but in the contest the poor woman fell from behind him, and was instantly murdered before his face; the female cannibals cutting her throat, and sucking her blood with as great a gust as though it had been wine. This done, they ripped her up and pulled out her entrails; with dismal fight sight caused the man to make the more resistance. It pleased providence, while he was engaged, twenty or thirty came together in a body; on which Sawney Beane and his blood-thirsty crew withdrew, and made the best of their Way through a thick Wood to their Den.

The man was the first that ever fell in their Way, that came off alive; he told the company what had happened, and showed them the body of his mangled wife, which the murderers had dragged out of the road, but had no time to carry off. They were struck with amazement, and went immediately to the Provost in Glasgow, who immediately sent to the King.

In a few Days his Majesty in Person, with a Body of about four hundred men, set out for the place where these tragedies were acted, in order to find out this hellish Crew which had so long been a Nuisance to that Part of the Kingdom.

The man who had been attacked was the guide, and care was taken to have a vast number of blood-hounds, that no possible means might be wanting to put an end to these barbarous cruelties.

No sign of humanity was found for a long time; and even when they came to the cave of those wretches, they took no notice of it, but were going to pursue their search along the shore, the tide being then out; but some of the blood hounds quickly entered into this cave and set up such a hedious barking howling and yelping, that the King and his attendance came back and looked into it, but did not think that anything human could there be concealed. Nevertheless as the blood hounds went farther in, they increased their noise, and refused to come back; torches were then immediately ordered, and a great many men entered thro' the most intricate windings, 'till they came to the private recess of the murderers.

The whole body then went in, and saw the dismal sight and were ready to sink into the earth to see such a number of arms, legs, thighs, hands and feet of men, women and children, hung up in rows like dry'd beef, and a great many laying in pickle. They also found a quantity of money, watches, rings, swords, pistols, a large quantity of cloathes, and other things which had been taken from those they murdered.

Sawney's family at this time consisted of himself, his wife, eight sons, six daughters, eighteen grand-sons, and fourteen grand-daughters, begotten in incest.

They were all seiz'd and pin-iron'd; and then they took what human flesh they found and buried it in the sands; and taking all the spoils, they returned to Edinburgh, with the prisoners, the country flocking round to see this cursed tribe. When they came to Edinburgh, they were all committed to the Talbooth and the next day conducted under strong guard to Lieth, where they were all executed without process, it being needless to try any creatures who were such professed enemies to mankind.

The men had first their privy members cut off, and thrown into the fire before their faces; then their hands and legs were cut off, by which amputation they bled to death in a few hours after.

The wife, daughters, and grand-children, having been made spectators of this just punishment inflicted on the men, were burnt to death in three several fires. They all died without the least sign of repentance, and continued venting the most horrid imprecations to the last gasp of life.[12]

The likeness to Captain Charles Johnson's printed edition is overwhelming, the differences are so scarce that they easily stand out. Intriguingly, the scene is set in 'Oalgay' instead of Galloway, and some historians accredit this to a location in Ireland and not Scotland—but given the references to Glasgow and Edinburgh, there is little doubt that this is nothing more than a spelling error, perhaps made by a person unfamiliar with the region.

Missing from this version—but present in Johnson's—are the limbs of the victims washing up on the shoreline and frightening the locals who came across them. Perhaps this was omitted to save space on the paper, given that the Aldermary Church version includes several woodcuts.

Also omitted were the details of how the Bean family staged their ambushes—surrounding their victims to ensure that none escaped alive. In contrast, Johnson gives a compelling amount of detail as to how they conducted their attacks. Why it is lacking in this edition is unknown.

The J. Ferraby Chapbook

J. Ferraby most likely printed his chapbook between 1815 and 1825, making it one of the earliest known chapbook editions of the Bean saga. This appears to be an earlier version because of the similarity with Johnson's account and its level of detail.

Like all chapbooks, it was designed to sensationalise as well as validate the authenticity of the tale, and does not provide the least bit of supporting evidence.

The Life of Sawney Beane
The Man-Eater

Who inhabited a cave near the Sea-Side in the Country of Galloway in Scotland, upwards of Twenty-five years

To which is added
The Droll Jester
Or
Laugh when you can

J. Ferraby, Printer, Butchery Hall.

The Life
Sawney Beane,

The Legend's Sordid Past

The following account, though as well attested as any historical fact can be, is almost incredible, for the monstrous and unparalleled barbarities it relates; there being nothing we have ever heard of, with the same degree of certainty, that can be compared with it; or that shows how far a brutal temper, untamed by education and a knowledge of the world, may carry a man in such glaring and horrible colours.

Sawney Beane was born in the county of East Lothian, about eight or nine miles eastward of the city of Edinburgh, some time in the reign of Queen Elizabeth whilst James I. governed only in Scotland. His parents worked at hedging and ditching for their livelihood, and brought up their son to the same occupation. He got his daily bread in his youth by these means; but soon contracting indolent habits and not caring to be confined to any honest employment, he left his mother and father, and ran away into the desert part of the country, taking with him a woman viciously inclined as himself.

These two took up their habitation in a rock by the sea side on the short of the country of Galloway, where they lived upwards of twenty five years, without going into any city, town or village.

In this time they had a great number of children and grand-children, whom they brought up after their own manner, without any notion of humanity or civil society. They never kept any company, but among themselves, and were supported entirely by robbery; being, more-over, so very cruel, that they never robbed any one whom they did not murder by which bloody method, and their being so retired from the world, they continued for a long time undiscovered there being no person able to guess how the people were lost that went by the place where they lived. As soon as they had robbed any man, woman, or child, they used to carry off the carcass to the den, where, cutting it into quarters, they would pickle the mangled limbs, and afterwards eat them; this being their only sustenance. And, notwithstanding they were at last so numerous, they commonly had a superfluity of this abominable food; so that in the night time they frequently threw legs and arms of the unhappy wretches they had murdered into the sea, at a great distance from their bloody habitat on; the limbs were often caste up by the tide in several parts of the country, to the astonishment and terror of beholders and others who were informed of it.

All people in the adjacent parts were at last alarmed at such an uncommon loss of their neighbours and acquaintance; for there was no travelling in safety near the den of these wretches; this occasioned the sending of frequent spies into the quarter, many of whom never returned again; and those who did, after the strictest enquiry, could not find how these melancholy matters happened. Several honest travellers were taken up on suspicion, and wrongfully hanged upon bare circumstances. Several innocent innkeepers were executed for no reason than that persons who had been thus lost, were known to have lain at their houses, which occasioned a suspicion of their being murdered by them, and their bodies privately buried in obscure places to prevent a discovery.

Thus an ill-placed justice was executed with the greatest severity imaginable, in order to prevent these frequent atrocious deeds; so that not a few inn-keepers, who lived on the western road of Scotland, left off their business, for fear of being made examples, and followed other employments. This on the other hand occasioned many great inconveniences to travellers, who were now in great distress for themselves and horses, when they were disposed to bait, or put up for lodging at night. In a word, the whole country was almost depopulated.

Still the Kings subjects were missing as much as before; so that it was the admiration of the whole kingdom how such villainies could be carried on, and the villains not be found out. A great many had been executed, and not one of them all had made any confession at the gallows; but stood to it to the last, that they were perfectly innocent of the crimes for which they suffered. When the magistrates found all in vain they left off these rigorous proceedings, and trusted wholly to kind Providence for the bringing to light of the authors of these unparalleled barbarities, when it should seem proper to the divine wisdom.

Sawney's family was at last grown very large, and every branch of it, as soon as able, assisted in perpetrating their wicked deeds, which they still followed with impunity. Sometimes they would attack four, five, or six footmen together; but never more than two if they were on horseback. They were, moreover, so careful, that not one they set upon should escape, that an ambuscade was placed on every side to secure them, let them fly which ever way they would, provided it should ever so happen that one or more got away from the first assailants. How was it possible that they would be detected, when not one that saw them ever saw any body else afterwards? The place which they inhabited was quite solitary and lonesome; and when the tide came up, the water went for near two hundred yards into their subterraneous habitation, which reached almost a mile under ground; so that when some, who had been sent armed to search all the by-places about, have past by the mouth of their cave, they have never taken notice of it, not supposing that any thing human would reside in such a place of perpetual darkness.

The number of the people these savages destroyed was never exactly known; but it was generally computed that in the twenty-five years they continued their butcheries, they had washed their hands in the blood of at least a thousand men, women, and children. The manner how they were at last discovered was as follows.

A man and his wife behind him on the same horse, coming home one evening from a fair, and falling into the ambuscade of these merciless wretches, they were fell upon them in the most furious manner. The man, for to save himself as well as he could, fought very bravely against them with sword and pistol, riding some of them down by main force of his horse. In the conflict the poor woman fell from behind him, and was instantly murdered before the husband's face; for the female cannibals cut her throat, and fell to sucking her blood as great a gust as if it had been wine. This being done they ripped up her belly, and pulled out entrails. Such a dreadful spectacle made the man make the more obstinate resistance, expecting the same fate if he fell into their hands. It pleased Providence, while he was engaged, that twenty or thirty from the same fair came together in a body; upon which Sawney Beane and his blood thirsty clan withdrew and made the best of their way through a thick wood to their den.

This man, who was the first that had ever fell in their way, and came off alive, told the whole company what had happened and showed them the horrid spectacle of his wife, whom the murderers had dragged to some distance, but had no time to carry her entirely off. They were struck with stupefaction and amazement at what he related, took him with them to Glasgow, and told the affair to the Provost of that city, who immediately sent to the King concerning it.

In about three or four days after, his majesty himself in person, with a body of about four hundred men, set out for the place where this dismal tragedy was acted, in order to search all the rocks and thickets, that if possible they might apprehend the hellish crew who had been so long pernicious to all the western parts of the kingdom.

The man who had been attacked was the guide; and care was taken to have a large number of blood-hounds with them, that no human means might be wanting to their putting an entire end of these cruelties.

No sign of habitation was to be found for a long time; and even when they came to the wretches' cave, they took not notice of it, but were going to pursue their search along the sea-shore, the tide being then out. But some of the blood-hounds luckily entered this Cimmerian den, and instantly set up a most hideous barking, howling, and yelping; so that the King, with his attendants, came back, and looked into it. They could not yet tell how to conceive that any thing human could be concealed in a place where they saw nothing but darkness. Nevertheless, as the blood hounds increased their noise, went father in, and refused to come back again, they began to imaging there was some reason more than ordinary.

Torches were now immediately sent for, and a great many men ventured in through the most intricate turnings and windings, till at last they arrived at that private recess from all the world, which was the habitation of these monsters.

Now the whole body, or as many of them as could, went in, and they were all so shocked at what they beheld, that they were almost ready to sink into the earth. Legs, arms, thighs, hands, and feet of men, women and children were hung in rows, like dried beef. A great many limbs lay in pickle; and a great mass of money, both gold and silver, with watches, rings, swords, pistols, and a large quantity of clothes, both linen and woollen, and an infinite number of other things taken from those whom they had murdered were thrown together in heaps or hung up against the sides of the den.

Sawney's family at this time, besides himself, consisted of his wife, eight sons, six daughters, eighteen grandsons and grand-daughters, who were all begotten in incest. These were all seized and pinioned by his majesty's order, in the first place; then they took what human flesh they had found and buried it in the sands; afterwards loading themselves with the spoils which they found, they returned to Edinburg with their prisoners; all the country as they passed along flocking to see this cursed tribe. When they were come to their journey's end, the wretches were all committed to the Tolbooth, from whence they were the next day conducted under a strong guard to Leith, were they all executed without any process, it being thought needless to try such enemies to mankind.

The men had first their privy members cut off, and thrown into the fire before their faces; then their hands and legs were severed from their bodies; by which amputation, they bled to death in some hours. The wife, daughters, and grand-children, having been made spectators of the punishment inflected on the men were afterwards burnt to death in three separate fires. They all died without the least sign of repentance; but continued cursing and venting the most dreadful imprecations to the very last gasp of life.[13]

It is clear that this version of the story was taken from the same source as that of Captain Charles Johnson's, if not lifted directly from Johnson's book. If anything, the text is more contemporary in its grammar and spelling, which adds weight to the idea of its succeeding the chapbook that followed Johnson's text. For example, it restores the disposing of arms and legs into the sea, and the manner in which the Beans staged their ambushes—details missing from the Aldermary Church copy, but included by Johnson. Thus, the J. Ferraby chapbook dispenses with the Aldermary Church printing.

This woodcut shows the Tolbooth as it would have appeared had the Beans been held there.

The F. Jollie and Sons Edition

The F. Jollie and Sons' edition of Sawney Bean's saga, aside from being in a much crisper typeface, makes subtle changes to the story which are worth considering. It is estimated that the chapbook was printed at the earliest in 1815 and most probably towards 1825. While it is clear that the author of this edition was either using the J. Ferraby edition, another undiscovered chapbook, or Captain Charles Johnson's book as source material, the story has been altered; those parts that differ most from the preceding versions are marked in italics.

The HORRID LIFE
of
Sawney Beane

Bella, bella, horrida, bella.

An Atrocious
Robber & Assassin

Nec dura nec aspera nec rent
Mors sola fatetura quantula sunt hominum corpuscula

Carlisle:
Printed by F. Jollie and Sons.

The Horrid Life of Sawney Beane etc.

[N.B. the introductory paragraph in the Ferraby edition is not included here:]

Sawney Beane was born in the county of East Lothian, about eight or nine miles eastward of the city of Edinburgh, sometime in the reign of Queen Elizabeth, whilst James I. governed only in Scotland. His parents worked at hedging and ditching for their livelihood, and brought up their son in the same occupation.

He got his daily bread in his youth by these means; but soon contracting indolent habits and not caring to be confined to any honest employment, he left his father and mother and ran away to the desert part of the country, taking with him a woman viciously inclined as himself.

These two took up their habitation in a rock by the sea side, on the shore of the county of Galloway, where they lived upwards of twenty five years, without going into any city, town or village.

In this time they had a great number of children and grand-children, whom they brought up after their own manner, without any notion of humanity or civil society. They never kept company, but among themselves, and were supported entirely by robbery; being moreover, so very cruel, that they never robbed anyone whom they did not murder; by which bloody method, and their being so retired from the world, they continued for a long time undiscovered; there being no person to guess how the people were lost that went by the place where they lived. As soon as they had robbed any man, woman, or child, they used to carry off the carcass to the den, where, cutting it into quarters, they would pickle the mangled limbs, and afterwards eat them, this being their only sustenance. And, notwithstanding, they were at last so numerous, they commonly had a superfluity of this abominable food so that in the night time they frequently threw legs and arms of the unhappy wretches they had murdered into the sea, at a great distance from their bloody habitation; the limbs were often cast up by the tide in several parts of the country, to the astonishment and terror of beholders and others who were informed of it.

All people in the adjacent parts were at last alarmed at such uncommon loss of their neighbours and acquaintance; for there was no travelling in safety near the den of these wretches: this occasioned the sending of frequent spies into the quarter, many of whom never returned again, and those who did, after the strictest search and enquiry, could not find out how these melancholy matters happened.

Several honest travellers were taken up on suspicion and wrongfully hanged up on bare circumstances: many innocent innkeepers were executed for no other reason than that their persons who had been lost and were known to have put up at their houses, which occasioned a suspicion of their being murdered by them, and their bodies privately buried in obscure places, to prevent a discovery. Thus an ill-placed justice was executed with the greatest severity imaginable, in order to prevent these frequent atrocious deeds; for which many innkeepers who lived on the western road of Scotland, left off their business, for fear of being made examples of, and took to some other employment.

Still the king's subjects were missing as much as before so that it became the admiration of the whole kingdom how such villainies could be carried on and the perpetrators go undiscovered. A great many had been executed; but not one of them made any confession at the gallows, but to the last declared, of course, that they were perfectly innocent of the crimes for which they suffered.

When the magistrates found all was in vain, they left off these rigorous proceedings, and trusted wholly to Providence, for the bringing to light the authors of these unparalleled barbarities, when it should seem proper to the divine Wisdom.

Sawney's family had now grown very large and every branch of it, as soon as able, assisted in the tragedies, which were so constantly performed with impunity. Sometimes they would attack four, five, and six footmen together, but never more than two if they were on horseback: they were moreover so careful that none whom they set upon should escape, that an ambuscade was placed on every side to secure them, let them fly which way they would, provided it ever should happen that one or more got away from the first assailants. It was not possible for them to be detected, when not one that saw them ever saw any body else afterwards.

The place where they inhabited was quite solitary and lonesome, and when the tide flowed, the water went for near two hundred yards into their subterraneous habitation, which reached almost a mile under ground; so that, when people who have been sent armed, to search all the places about, have passed by the mouth of the cave, they have never taken the last notice of it, little supposing that any thing human would reside in such a place of perpetual horror and darkness.

The number of people the savages destroyed was never exactly known; but it was general computed that, in the twenty-five years they had continued their butcheries, they had washed their hands in the blood of thousands at least, men, women, and children.

But almighty Vengeance did not suffer these execrable monsters longer to go unpunished. A man with his wife behind him on the same horse, coming one evening home from a fair, and falling into Sawney's ambuscade, was attacked in the most furious manner., The man, to save himself as well he could, fought very bravely against them with sword and pistol, riding some of them down by main force of his horse.

In the conflict the poor woman fell from behind him, and was instantly murdered before her husband's face; for the female cannibals cut her throat, and fell to sucking her blood with as great a gust as if it had been wine; this done, they ripped up her belly and pulled out all her entrails. Such a dreadful spectacle made the man a more obstinate resistance, as expecting the same fate if he had fallen into their hands; and, providentially, while he was thus employed, thirty or forty people, coming from the same fair, made their appearance; which obliged Sawney and his blood-thirsty clan to withdraw, and make the best of their way through the thick wood to their den.

In about three or four days after, his majesty himself, at the head of four hundred men, set out for the place where this dismal tragedy was acted, in order to search all of the rocks and thickets, that, if possible, might apprehend this hellish crew, which, had so long been the terror of the western part of the kingdom. The man who had been attacked, was their guide, and care was taken to have a large number of bloodhounds with them, that no human means might be wanting towards putting an end to these cruelties.

No sign of any habitation was to be found for a long time; and even when they came to the cave, they took no notice of it, but were going to pursue their search along the sea-shore, the tide being then out; but some of the bloodhounds luckily entered the Cimmerian den, and instantly set up a most hideous barking.

Now the whole body, or as many of them could, went in, and were so terrified at what they beheld, that they began to imagine themselves in another world. Legs, arms, thighs, hands and feet of men, women, and children, were hung up in rows like dried beef, a great many limbs lay in pickle, and heaps of money, both gold and silver, with rings, watches, swords, pistols and a large quantity of clothes, and an infinite number of other things, which they had taken from those whom they had murdered.

Sawney's family, at this time, besides himself, consisted of his wife, eight sons, six daughters, eighteen grandsons, and fourteen granddaughters; which, after a slight resistance, were all taken and safely bound. The solders then collected what human flesh they could find and buried in the sands, afterwards, loading themselves with the spoils which they found, they returned to Edinburgh with their prisoners; all the country, as they passed along, flocking to see this cursed tribe.

When they came to the journey's end, the wretches were all committed to the Tolbooth, from whence they were conducted, under a strong guard, to Leith, where they were executed without any process; it being thought needless to try creatures who were professed enemies of mankind.

The men were dismembered, their hands and legs were severed from their bodies; by which amputations they were suffered to bleed to death. The wife, daughters and grandchildren, being made spectators of this just punishment, inflicted on the men, were burnt to death in three separate fires. They all died without the least sign of contrition, and continued cursing, and uttering the most dreadful imprecations to the last breath.

> NEQUE SEMPER ARCUM TENDIT APOLLO.
> *Neither does Apollo always bend his bow.*[14]

While essentially the same story, this second edition presents some dramatic departures worth considering. Firstly, the removal of any direct references to the incest: Sawney and his family simply exist, and no hint is given as to how their numbers grew. The reader is informed that they had no contact with the outside world, so is left to wonder whether incest was involved, or whether some of the victims were taken prisoner and forced to copulate with the Beans. While the incest is implied, it is omitted.

Secondly, the introduction to the story from the J. Ferraby edition has been omitted. This is odd, because that paragraph provides the moral context for the story, and this chapbook does emphasise religious undertones. Additions such as 'But almighty Vengeance did not suffer these execrable monsters longer to go unpunished' imply a greater concern for incorporating Christian morality in the story on the part of F. Jollie and Sons. Another potential example may be the retelling of the Bean men's execution: all prior (and many later) editions of the story refer to the men's privy members being cut off, but this detail is excluded from this edition. Was this done for a more puritanical reading community, or was this censorship merely the editor imposing his own literary taste onto the story?

Also omitted are the finer details of the apprehension of the Bean clan, the mention of Glasgow, and the trek to take the Beans back to Edinburgh—but we have no way of knowing if these were cut due to space considerations or with another purpose in mind.

The S. & T. Martin Chapbook

This edition is held in the British Library and was printed in Birmingham by S. & T. Martin Printers, who dealt in penny chapbooks and operated between 1807 and 1810. This version, transcribed in Appendix C, mirrors many of the other chapbooks, and most prominently the Aldermary Church Yard chapbook, for it too misspells Galloway 'Oalgay'. However, it has at least one glaring error.

Aside from subtle differences in wording and sentence structure, the S. & T. Martin chapbook misquotes, 'The place they inhabited was solitary and lonesome; and when the tide came up, it went near two Hundred miles under ground: so that when some have been sent armed, they have passed by the mouth of the cave without any notice; not supposing that a human creature could reside in such a place of horror.'[15] Instead of a cavern that was two hundred *yards* deep, the authors envisioned one that would stretch from the west coast of Scotland all the way to Edinburgh!

Beyond this one difference, however, this edition is unremarkable, nor does it add any details to the crime or the alleged criminals.

Other Related Chapbooks

It is impossible to examine the Sawney Bean chapbooks without exploring other works of this genre. Is it possible that the legend was coloured by other chapbook digest? Could some of its variations target people other than the Scottish?

A review of the chapbook collections of the National Library of Scotland and the British Library reveals at least two stories— featuring the villains John M'Claud, Joseph Franks, and John Gregg—potentially related to Sawney Bean's tale. The following is another short story on cannibalism.

> The Dreadful History of John M'Claud And His Crew of Thieves, Robbers and Murderers Who were taken in a cave, near by the Sea-Side, in Devonshire, where they haunted for twenty-five Years, without being found out, as they had different Inlets to this Cave, and robbed about 800 People.
>
> How they were taken, condemned, and executed at Plymouth; with their Behaviour when hanged and burnt.
>
> A wonderful Relation of JOSEPH FRANKS, and seven other Savages, Taken in the Mountains of Hungary, who killed more than Eighty Persons, and eat the human Flesh of those they murdered.

The following history is the strongest evidence of horrid barbarity ever known for these four hundred years past. And, were it not well attested by Ministers, Deacons, and Wardens, few could credit there were such creatures on the earth, so as to be capable to eat human flesh. True it is, that in the Dutch and Portuguese settlements near the Cape of Good Hope, there are Cannibals who eat human bodies and all sorts of carrion, and wears the tripes of them round their legs and arms, paints their bodies with the tallow or grease of the same. But in this quarter of the globe there are no such monsters known. This cove and rock in Cornwall, those who knew them and their situation, affirm, that many villains have frequented them time out of memory. But as there is orders put out for twelve men, on the charge of the country, to search that place once a day, and to take up all travellers, on account of the turnpike road which goes very near it, and about six miles from any inhabitants; so that this will put an end to their lurking den.

The Dying Words of John M'Claud.

The following account, though as well attested as any historical fact can be, is almost incredible, for the monstrous and unparalleled barbarities that it relates, there being nothing in novels we ever heard of with the same degree of certainty, that may be compared with it or that shows how far a brutish temper, untamed by education and knowledge of the world, may carry a man to such glaring and horrible colours.

John M'Claud was born in the County of Devonshire, about eight or nine miles eastward of the city of Exeter, his parents worked at hedging and ditching for their livelihood, and brought up their son to the same occupation. He got his daily bread in his youth by the these means, but being very much addicted to idleness, and not choosing to be confined to any honest employment, he left his father and mother, and run away into the desart parts of the country, with a woman as viciously inclined as himself, of Devonshire, where they lived upward of 25 years without going into any city, town or village.

During the course of this retirement, they associated themselves from time to time with a great number of abandoned profligates who had been brought up after their own manner, without the least notion of humanity or civil society; they never kept any other company, and supported themselves by robbing, being moreover, so very cruel that they never robbed any one but they murdered.

By this bloody method, and their living so retired from the world, they continued a long time undiscovered, there being no body able to guess how the people were lost, who went by the place where they lived. As soon as they robbed and murdered any man, woman or child they used to carry off their carcasses to their den, where cutting them in quarters, they would pickle the mangled limbs and eat them, it being soustenance. All the people, in the adjacent parts, were alarmed at so uncommon a loss of their neighbours; for there was no traveling near the den of these wretches. The occasional spies to be sent into those parts, many of them never returning again; those that did, after the strictest search and enquiry, could not find out how these melancholy matters happened; there were several honest travellers taken up upon suspicion and wrongfully hanged; several innocent innkeepers were executed for no other reason than that they persons who had been lost were known to have lain at their houses, and their bodies privately buried in obscure places. Thus an ill placed justice, was executed with the greatest severity imaginable, in order to prevent these frequent atrocious deeds, that the innkeepers who lived on the western roads left of their business for fear of being made examples of, and followed other employments. This, on the other hand, occasioned many great inconveniences to passengers, who were now in great distress for want of accommodation for themselves and their horses when they were disposed to bait, or put up for lodgings at night; in a word, the whole country was depopulated.

Thus did John and his abominable Gang go on in their unheard villainies, perpetuating their wicked deeds, which they followed with impunity. Some times they would attack four, five or six footmen together, but never more than two if on horseback. They were also very careful none should escape, am ambuscade being on every side to secure them every way; how then was it possible they should be detected, when not one that saw them ever perceived any body afterwards? The place they inhabited was solitary and lonesome, and when the tide came up, it reached a mile under ground, so that when some had been sent armed, they passed by the mouth of the cave without any notice, not supposing that any human would live in such a place of horror.

The number of people they destroyed was never known; but it was computed that in 25 years they had murdered 800 men, women and children. And the manner they were discovered was as follows.

A farmer and his wife behind him, on the same horse, coming one evening home from a fair and falling into an ambuscade of these wretches, they attacked him in a furious manner. The man to save himself, fought bravely, riding some of them down by main force; but in the conflict the poor woman fell from behind him, and was instantly murdered before his face; the female canibals cutting her throat and sucking her blood with great gust as though it had been wine. This done, they ripped her up and pulled out her entrails, which dismal spectacle caused the man to make more resistance, it pleased Providence, while he was engaged that thirty people came in from a body together from a fair, on which

John M'Claud and his crew withdrew, and made the best of their way, through a wood, to their den.

This was the first man that fell in their way and came off alive; he told the company what had happened, and shewed them the mangled body of his wife which the murderers had not time to carry off. They were struck with amazement and went and made it known to the Mayor of Exeter, who sent an express to the high sheriff of the county, who assembled together about 400 of the country people, who set out for the place where these tragedies were acted in order to find out the hellish crew which so long had been a nuisance to that part of the kingdom. The man that had been attacked was the guide. No sign of the habitation was found for a long time, and even when they came to the cave of these wretches, they took no notice of it, but were going for to pursue their search along the shore, the tide being then out, torches were immediately had, and a great many men entered through the intricate windings, till they came to the private Recess of the murderers; they also found a quantity of money, watches, rings, swords, pistols, and a large quantity of cloaths, which they had taken from those they had murdered.

John's savage gang, in the whole, consisted of fifty in number; and they were all seized and pinioned, and they took what human flesh they found and buried it in the sands; then taking all the spoil, they returned to Exeter, with the prisoners, the country people flocking round to see the cursed tribe. When they came to the town, they were committed to the goal, and the next day conducted under strong guard to Plymouth, and in three days tried and condemned. Their sentence was awful, eleven men and ten women received sentence of death, the men were strangled, their bodies dissected, their privy members with their legs and arms cut off—The women, with their daughters, were strangled and burnt, dying without the least sign of repentance, and were consumed cursing and swearing, uttering the most horrid imprecations, to the last gasp of their breath. Thus ended a scene of misery, the greatest ever seen in Britain, or any Christian nation.—Canibals were never known in this kingdom before, yet the attestation here annexed, is so strong, it makes this horrible scene extraordinary.

This was printed in the desire of William Williams, George Abecromby, John Cashon, Sheriffs,

JOSEPH FRANKS.
And Seven other Savages.

Of eight wonderful Savages taken in the mountain of Hungary in February last, who lived in a hole in the middle of a mountain, and killed most of the travellers who came on the roads, and eat their flesh. Above eighty were killed an eaten, and salted in their hold, when they were taken, and very much treasure was likewise found. Many chapmen carriers and postboys were murdered and eaten. In a word, many travellers were barbarously murdered by these savages; for as they sleeped in these mountains for fifteen years, the country was in terror, as they supposed there were wolves, tygers, and other ravenous beasts in the mountains. The country hereupon rose, in order to search those mountains, when they came upon those canibals and took them, and they have received the just reward of their cruelty.

FINIS[16]

First and foremost, the John M'Claud chapbook bears striking resemblances to the Sawney Bean legend, and in many parts reads as though it has been lifted from the Sawney Bean chapbook word for word—or, perhaps, vice versa. The National Library of Scotland estimates that this document was published around 1800, fifteen years prior to the Sawney Bean chapbook. This indicates that, after Captain Charles Johnson's book, the John M'Claud story may have appeared next, which would then have been followed by the Beans chapbooks.

The elements that the two stories have in common are numerous:

The amount of time that the story covers—in this case, twenty-five years.
The opening paragraph is almost identical to the J. Ferraby chapbook of Sawney Bean.
Both Sawney and John M'Claud are Scottish.
Both men begin their lives in a family of hard-working parents ('hedging and ditching') but both were idle.
Both Sawney and M'Claud fall in with vicious women who remain unnamed.
None of their victims live to tell the tale for over twenty-five years.
Both Bean and M'Claud's gangs/families engage in pickling and eating their victims.
Spies are sent to root out the murderers, but fail to locate them.
Innocent innkeepers are mistaken for the culprits and killed.
The structure of the Beans' and M'Clauds' ambush attacks are almost identical.
Both the Beans and M'Clauds live in caves.
Bean and M'Claud's downfalls come when an innocent farmer and his wife are brutally attacked and the farmer escapes.
Once captured, the men are put to death in almost exactly the same way (bled and burned).

Despite their similarities, the stories diverge in the following points:

Sawney and his clan are said to have killed 1,000, whereas the M'Clauds are only responsible for 800 murders.
The M'Claud story takes place in Devonshire in England.
There only indication of when the M'Claud story takes place appears at the end of the story, where the allusion to three sheriffs hints at a contemporary setting; Bean's tale is firmly situated in the time of James I's reign.
The Mayor of Exeter, and not the king, launches the manhunt in the M'Claud story.
M'Claud's gang is larger than Bean's—it is fifty strong.
M'Claud's gang does not appear to be the product of incest, but is staffed with 'abandoned profligates'.
M'Claud is not executed in Leith or in Edinburgh, but in Plymouth.

There is still a Scottish undercurrent to the tale—in the name of the perpetrator, John M'Claud. Other than that, the story is repositioned for the reading public as an English tale of horrific crime. If indeed the purpose of the Bean legend is to slander the Scottish people, the same cannot be said here. One explanation is that the author who lifted this tale from Captain Charles Johnson's account may not have had the same intention as the latter; and if slander of the Scottish was intended, why would the author not preserve the character of Bean and his Galwegian surroundings?

The M'Claud chapbook is equally interesting because it introduces another cannibalistic tale, that of John Franks. While the story is short and rudimentary in its detail, it does confer readers with the impression that cannibalism was prevalent, thus lending credibility to the M'Claud story.

Another fascinating element is the accreditation of three sheriffs at the end of the chapbook: 'This was printed in the desire of William Williams, George Abecromby, John Cashon, Sheriffs'. This could have been printed to make the public aware of the kind of crime that they were engaged in policing, and adds credibility of the tale besides. A survey of local genealogy groups, however, has not yielded any record of these three sheriffs. While it is possible that their names and occupations were simply not recorded at the time, it is more likely that this was a bit of fiction to add weight to the story.

There is no historical evidence to support the tale of John M'Claud. It only appears in chapbook form, its only known print. Like the Bean story, evidence to support the tale does not exist in documented form.

The Tale of John Gregg

Another chapbook related to the Sawney Bean's story is *The History of John Gregg, and his Family, of Robbers and Murderers*. This story was printed in 1789, which brings it closer to Captain Charles Johnson's tale. The similarities between John Gregg and Sawney Bean are too numerous to mention, but there are a handful of differences. To comprehend the role of this story, we must first digest it!

> The History of John Gregg, and his Family, of Robbers and Murders.
>
> Who took up their abode in a cave near to the sea-side, in Clovaley in Devonshire, where they liv'd twenty-five years without so much as once going to visit any city, or town. How they robbed above one thousand persons, and murdered and ate, all whom they robbed. How at last they were happily discovered by a pack of bloodhounds; and how John Gregg, his wife, eight sons, six daughters, eighteen grand-sons, and fourteen grand-daughters, were all seized and executed, by being cast alive into three fires, and burnt.
>
> The following account, tho' as well attested as any historical fact can be, is almost incredible, for monstrous and unparalleled barbarities; that in novels there is nothing that we have ever heard of with the same degree of certainty that may be compared with it; or that shews how brutish temper, untamed by education and knowledge of the world, may carry a man in such glaring and horrible actions.
>   John Gregg was born in the county of Devon, about eight or nine miles eastward of the city of Exeter. His parents worked at hedging and ditching for their livelihood, and brought their son up to the same occupation. He got his daily bread in his youth by these means; but being very addicted to idleness, and not chusing to be confined to any honest employment, he left his father and mother, and ran away into the desart part of the country, taking with him a woman, as viciously inclined as himself, these two took their habitation in a Rock by the Sea-side on the short of the county of Devon, where they lived upwards of twenty-five years without going into any city, town or village.
>   In this time they had a great number of children and grand-children whom they brought up after their own manner, without the least notion of humanity or civil society. They never kept any company but among themselves, and supported themselves by robbing, being moreover so very cruel, that they never robbed any one but what they murdered.

By this blood method and living so retired from the world, they continued a long time undiscovered, there being nobody able to guess how the people were lost who went by the place where they lived. As soon as they had robbed and murdered any man, woman or child they used to carry off their carcases to their den, where cutting them into quarters, they would pickle their mangled limbs, and afterwards eat them, it being their subsistence.

All the people in the adjacent parts were alarmed at so uncommon a loss of their neighbours; for there was no travelling near the den of these wretches. This occasioned spies to be sent into these parts, many of whom never returned again, and those who did, after the strictest search and enquiry could not find out how these melancholy matters happened. There were several honest travellers taken up upon suspicion, and wrongfully hanged; several innocent innkeepers were executed for no other reasons than that the persons who had been lost were known to have lain at their houses, which occasioned suspicion of their being murdered by them, and their bodies privately buried in obscure places to prevent discovery. Thus an ill-placed Justice was executed within the greatest severity imaginable, in order to prevent these frequent atrocious deeds, that the innkeepers, who lived on the western road, left off their business for fear of being made examples of, and followed other employments; this on the other hand occasioned many great inconveniences to passengers, who were now in very great distress for what of accommodation for themselves and their horses, when they were disposed to bait or put up for lodging at night. In a word, the whole country was depopulated.

John's family was at last grown very large, and every branch, as soon as able, assisted in perpetuating their wicked deeds, which they followed with impunity: sometimes they would attack four, five, or six footmen together, but never more than two if on horseback. They were also very careful that none should escape, an ambuscade being laid on every side to secure them every way, how then it was possible they should be detected, when not one that saw them ever perceived any body afterwards? The place they inhabited was solitary and lonesome, and when the tide came up, it reached a mile under ground, so that when some had been sent armed, they passed by the mouth of the cave without any notice, not supposing anything human would live in such a place of horror.

The number of people they destroyed was never known, but it was computed in twenty-five years they had murdered one thousand men, women, and children, and the manner they were discovered was as follows.

A man and his wife behind him on the same horse coming home from a fair, and falling into the ambuscade of these wretches, they attacked him in a furious manner: The man to save himself fought bravely, riding some of them down by main force, but in the conflict, the poor woman fell from behind him and was instantly murdered before his face, the female cannibals cutting her throat, and sucking her blood with as great gust, as tho' it had been wine. This done, they ripp'd her up and pull'd out her entrails; which dismal spectacle caused the man to make the more resistance. It pleased Providence, while he was engag'd, thirty people came in a body together from the fair; on which John Gregg and his crew withdrew, and made the best of their way thro' a wood to their den.

This was the first man that ever fell in their way and came off alive. He told the company what had happened and show'd the mangled body of his wife, which the murderers had not time to carry off. They were struck with amazement, and went and made it known to the Mayor of Exeter, who immediately sent to the king. In a few days his Majesty in person with a body of four hundred men, set out for the place where these tragedies were acted, in order to find out this hellish crew, which so long had been a nuisance to that part of the Kingdom. The man who had been attacked was the guide, and care was taken to have a large number of blood hounds, that no human means might be wanting to put an end to those barbarous cruelties. No sign of habitation was found for a long time and even when they came to the cave of these wretches, they took not notice of it, but were going to pursue their search along the shore, the tide being then out; but some of the blood hounds luckily entered the cave, and set up such a hideous barking and yowling, that the king and his attendants went back and looked to it, but could not think that any thing human was there. Nevertheless, as the hounds went further in, they increased their noise and refused to come back; torches were immediately had, and a great many men entered thro' the most intricate windings, 'till they came to the private recess of the murderers: then the whole body of them went in, and saw the dismal sight, and were ready to sink into the earth er to see such a multitude of arms, legs, thighs, hands and feet of men, women, and children, hung up in rows, like dry'd beef and a great many lying in pickle. They also found a quantity of money, watches, rings swords, pistols, and a large quantity of cloathes and other things, which they had taken from those they had murdered.

John's family at this time consisted of himself, his wife, eight sons, six daughters, eighteen grand-sons, and fourteen grand-daughters, begotten in incest: they then were all seized and pinioned; they took what human flesh they found and buried it in the sands, then taking all the spoil, they returned to Exeter with the prisoners, the country people flocking round to see the cursed tribe. When they came to the town, they were committed to the goal, and the next day conducted under a strong guard to Plymouth, where they were executed without any process, it being needless to try any creatures who were such prosess'd enemies to mankind.

The men had first their privy members cut off and thrown into the fire before their faces; and then their hands and legs were cut off, by which amputation they bled to death some hours afterwards.

The wife, daughters and grand-children having been made spectators of this just punishment inflicted on the men, were burnt to death in three several fires. They all dy'd without the least sign of repentance, and continued cursing and swearing the most horrid Imprecations to the last gasp of breath.

FINIS

Printed in Glasgow [17]

John Gregg and Sawney Bean's stories are identical but for their locations, for Gregg lives outside of the county of Devon, east of Exeter—like in the story of John M'Claud. Also like in the latter, the Mayor of Exeter is the man to hunt down these criminals, and there is no clue of the time in which these events occurred.

This chapbook has no ties to Scotland, however, perhaps because it was printed in Glasgow. If anything, Scottish retaliation may have been at play here, recasting the Beans as an English abomination.

As to the validity of the tale, historian Peter Christie provides the most succinct explanation in his research of the North Devon Savages:

> Another group of references to 'wild' people in Devon comes from the field of fiction (allowing that the Gubbins were based on some sort of reality). The earliest fiction reference is from a broadsheet entitled, *The HISTORY of John Gregg and his FAMILY of Robbers and Murderers*. This Gregg was said to have lived at Clovelly and eaten those whom he first robbed. The broadsheet has recently been reprinted as a pamphlet but its claims for a Devon locale are extremely tenuous. It seems clear that it is just a cheapjack copy of the much better-known Sawney Bean story centred in Scotland and dating to the eighteenth century.[18]

The Bloody Innkeeper

A five-page chapbook printed in 1675, *The Bloody Innkeeper; or Sad and Barbarous News from Gloucester-shire: Being A True Relation how the Bodies of Seven Men and Women were found Murthered in a Garden belonging to a House in Putley, near Glocester. With the strange and miraculous manner how the same was discovered by a Smith that lately took the House, digging to set up his Anvil, and finding a Knife in one of the Bodies*, may well have contributed as a potential source of the Sawney Bean tale. It is the story of a couple—a Cromwellian soldier and his Scottish wife—who ran an inn in the village of Putley, on the road between Gloucester and Bristol. Their business was not very successful—'otherwise very small and inconsiderable'[19]—yet in spite of this, they thrived financially—'contrary to all expectations, they began to thrive amain, furnishing their house rarely well with all sorts of Household goods and convenient Utensils'.[20] After several years of running their little inn, they moved their operation to Gloucester.

A blacksmith set up shop in their former home, and while digging up part of the garden, he discovered the bodies of seven men and women. It became clear that the innkeepers had been murdering and robbing their guests. The couple 'was swel'd with blood, and [their] Gaines raked together with the Barbarous hands of Robbery and Murther'; one of their victims still had a rusting blade embedded in his chest.[21]

In *The Bloody Innkeeper*, innkeepers are once more suspected of evil deeds, although—unlike in the Bean saga—here this proves to be correct; like the Beans, they are serial killers; and finally, the Innkeeper's wife is Scottish.

Summary—Was Sawney Intended to Insult The Scottish People?

It is nearly impossible to get into the mind of the author of this story when we know nothing about him. Whether 'Sawney' or 'M'Claud', the name of the chief villain retains a decisively Scottish inflection. The only variation of the story that does not cast the Scots in a suspect light is the chapbook on John Gregg, which was printed on Glasgow. Other stories of the era such as *The Bloody Innkeeper* garnish the villainous characters with ties to Scotland—perhaps playing off contemporary stereotypes or catering to popular demand. Even if the intent wasn't there, the result was the association of the Scottish—to various degrees—with the grotesque, and inhumane.

4

The Beans Go Mainstream

The Newgate Calendar was one of those books, along with a Bible, Foxe's Book of Martyrs and the Pilgrim's Progress, most likely to be found in any English home between 1750 and 1850. Children were encouraged to read it because it was believed to inculcate principles of right living—by fear of punishment if not by the dull and earnest morals appended to the stories of highwaymen and other felons.[1]

The era of the chapbook came to an end as relatively affordable hardbound books became more prevalent. The chapbooks didn't entirely die, for the essence of this genre was transported to the medium of printed books—such was the case of Sawney Bean. His story was adapted in the guise of the *Newgate Calendars*, through which Sawney's murderous family grew in readership and credibility.

The Newgate Calendars

The calendars reference the Newgate prison, the largest institution of its type in London, an annex of the Old Bailey—the Central Criminal Court. The series of *Newgate Calendars* derived from several sources, the first of which were the Sessions papers of the trials held at the Old Bailey starting around 1730. Some of the books referred to Tyburn, which was the traditional execution site for London, approximately two miles from the Newgate, and common chapbooks also furnished them with material.

The legal proceedings, the official accounts of murder trials, and their outcomes were often filled with sordid tales of murder, gore, and obscenity. It was not uncommon to include true confessions, or a killer's last dying words, which were very popular with readers. The authors of the *Newgate Calendars* referred to themselves as editors, and often wrote anonymously. Research has revealed that most of they were penned by prison chaplains with ready access to the criminals: the tone of many stories does have strike a moral chord, and chaplains would have been among the few people allowed to witness the confessions or last utterances of criminals.

It is important to note that the *Newgate Calendars* were not published by a single party and in fact designated a genre more than they did a coherent series. As such, 'Newgate Calendar' can refer to any of a plethora of works listed in Appendix D.

The *Newgate Calendars* had certain recurring themes, not least a moral design. The editors were obviously attempting to dissuade people from a life of crime, so while readers could relish in the gory details, the conclusion remained that crime didn't pay: the guilty were always pursued, caught, tried, and convicted. If the authors are to be believed, most felons came to the realisation that the criminal life was wrong. Their punishment, however much deserved, was always swift and brutal—often execution at Tyburn.

The opening of each book so entitled is distinguished by the woodcut of a stately mother sitting in a chair, clutching her own copy of the *Newgate Calendar* while a young child stands at her side. The mother is pointing out the window to a figure on a hill, hanging by the gallows. Under each woodcut reads the caption:

Illustration of each *Newgate Calendar*.

The anxious Mother with a Parents Care,
Presents our Labours to her future Heir
'The Wise, the Brave, the temperate and the Just,
Who love their neighbour, and in God who trust
Safe through the Dang'rous paths of Life may Steer,
Nor dread those Evils we exhibit Here'.[3]

There is little room for misinterpretation: if you didn't heed the tales in the *Newgate Calendar*, you would end up at the gallows yourself. To eighteenth- and nineteenth-century readers, the *Newgate Calendars* were books of great moral significance.

Yet crime was booming in this era: public executions were widely attended, and the execution crowds a thriving workplace for pickpockets; drinking and brawling were commonplace among spectators on the prisoner's route from the Newgate to Tyburn; apartment dwellers who lived along the road to the execution often rented their abodes out for parties who wanted a better view; and young apprentices were often sent by their employers to witness the executions to discourage them from a life of crime.[4] At the executions of famous criminals, work in London all but ground to a halt amid a morbidly festive atmosphere.

The Newgate prison itself was a source of income. The facility was often overcrowded, since it did not deal with long-term prisoners, and acted more as a provisional stop on the way to the gallows. The accommodation—especially in the lower levels—was filthy, disease-ridden, and rodent infested. But despite the harsh conditions, some cells were much cleaner and dryer that others, so the head jailer charged rent to the prisoners accordingly, making his a coveted position that he in turn had to pay for. Those inmates who could afford it spent their money on better facilities, and those who couldn't were shunted to the most dismal cells. Thus became the Newgate a bizarre hotel of sorts, which nonetheless catered to the worst criminal elements in England.[5]

In any case, the *Newgate* variants of Captain Charles Johnson's story are much more editorially polished than those the Bean chapbooks.

Sawney Bean—The Newgate Calendars—1780:
SAWNEY BEAN
An incredible Monster who, with his Wife, lived by Murder and Cannibalism in a Cave. Executed at Leith with his whole Family in the Reign of James the First.

THE following account, though as well attested as any historical fact can be, is almost incredible; for the monstrous and unparalleled barbarities

The Newgate Prison.

that it relates; there being nothing that we ever heard of, with the same degree of certainty, that may be compared with it, or that shows how far a brutal temper, untamed by education, may carry a man in such glaring and horrible colours.

Sawney Bean was born in the county of East Lothian, about eight or nine miles eastward of the city of Edinburgh, some time in the reign of Queen Elizabeth, whilst King James I. governed only in Scotland. His parents worked at hedging and ditching for their livelihood, and brought up their son to the same occupation. He got his daily bread in his youth by these means, but being very much prone to idleness, and not caring for being confined to any honest employment, he left his father and mother, and ran away into the desert part of the country, taking with him a woman as viciously inclined as himself. These two took up their habitation in a cave, by the seaside on the shore of the county of Galloway, where they lived upwards of twenty five years without going into any city, town, or village.

In this time they had a great number of children and grandchildren, whom they brought up after their own manner, without any notions of humanity or civil society. They never kept any company, but among themselves, and supported themselves wholly by robbing; being, moreover, so very cruel, that they never robbed anyone whom they did not murder.

By this bloody method, and their living so retiredly from the world, they continued such a long time undiscovered, there being nobody able to guess how the people were lost that went by the place where they lived. As soon as they had robbed and murdered any man, woman or child, they used to carry off the carcass to the den, where, cutting it into quarters, they would pickle the mangled limbs, and afterwards eat it; this being their only sustenance. And, notwithstanding, they were at last so numerous, they commonly had superfluity of this their abominable food; so that in the night time they frequently threw legs and arms of the unhappy wretches they had murdered into the sea, at a great distance from their bloody habitation. The limbs were often cast up by the tide in several parts of the country, to the astonishment and terror of all the beholders, and others who heard of it.

Persons who had gone about their lawful occasions fell so often into their hands that it caused a general outcry in the country round about, no man knowing what was become of his friend or relation, if they were once seen by these merciless cannibals.

All the people in the adjacent parts were at last alarmed at such a common loss of their neighbours and acquaintance; for there was no travelling in safety near the den of these wretches. This occasioned the sending frequent spies into these parts, many of whom never returned again, and those who did, after the strictest search and inquiry, could not find how these melancholy matters happened. Several honest travellers were taken up on suspicion, and wrongfully hanged upon bare circumstances; several innocent innkeepers were executed for no other reason than that persons who had been thus lost were known to have lain at their houses, which occasioned a suspicion of their being murdered by them and their bodies privately buried in obscure places to prevent a discovery. Thus an ill placed justice was executed with the greatest severity imaginable, in order to prevent these frequent atrocious deeds; so that not a few innkeepers, who lived on the Western Road of Scotland, left off their business, for fear of being made examples, and followed other employments. This on the other hand occasioned many great inconveniences to travellers, who were now in great distress for accommodation for themselves and their horses when they were disposed to refresh themselves and their horses, or put up for lodging at night. In a word, the whole country was almost depopulated.

Still the King's subjects were missing as much as before; so that it was the admiration of the whole kingdom how such villainies could be carried on and the perpetrators not discovered. A great many had been executed, and not one of them all made any confession at the gallows, but stood to it at the last that they were perfectly innocent of the crimes for which they suffered. When the magistrates found all was in vain, they left off these rigorous proceedings, and trusted wholly to Providence for the bringing to light the authors of these unparalleled barbarities, when it should seem proper to the Divine wisdom.

Sawney's family was at last grown very large, and every branch of it, as soon as able, assisted in perpetrating their wicked deeds, which they still followed with impunity. Sometimes they would attack four, five or six foot men together, but never more than two if they were on horseback. They were, moreover, so careful that not one whom they set upon should escape, that an ambuscade was placed on every side to secure them, let them fly which way they would, provided it should ever so happen that one or more got away from the first assailants. How was it possible they should be detected, when not one that saw them ever saw anybody else afterwards? The place where they inhabited was quite solitary and lonesome; and when the tide came up, the water went for near two hundred yards into their subterraneous habitation, which reached almost a mile underground; so that when people, who had been sent armed to search all the places about had passed by the mouth of their cave, they had never taken any notice of it, not supposing that anything human would reside in such a place of perpetual horror and darkness.

The number of the people these savages destroyed was never exactly known, but it was generally computed that in the twenty-five years they continued their butcheries they had washed their hands in the blood of a thousand, at least, men, women and children. The manner how they were at last discovered was as follows.

A man and his wife behind him on the same horse coming one evening home from a fair, and falling into the ambuscade of these merciless wretches, they fell upon them in a most furious manner. The man, to save himself as well as he could, fought very bravely against them with sword and pistol, riding some of them down, by main force of his horse. In the conflict the poor woman fell from behind him, and was instantly murdered before her husband's face; for the female cannibals cut her throat and fell to sucking her blood with as great a gust as if it had been wine. This done, they ripped up her belly and pulled out all her entrails. Such a dreadful spectacle made the man make the more obstinate resistance, as expecting the same fate if he fell into their hands. It pleased Providence, while he was engaged, that twenty or thirty from the same fair came together in a body; upon which Sawney Bean and his bloodthirsty clan withdrew, and made the best of their way through a thick wood to their den.

This man, who was the first that had ever fallen in their way and come off alive, told the whole company what had happened, and showed them the horrid spectacle of his wife, whom the murderers had dragged to some distance, but had not time to carry her entirely off. They were all struck with stupefaction and amazement at what he related, took him with them to Glasgow, and told the affair to the provost of that city, who immediately sent to the King concerning it. In about three or four days after, his Majesty himself in person, with a body of about four hundred men, set out for the place where this dismal tragedy was acted, in order to search all the rocks and thickets, that, if possible, they might apprehend this hellish crew, which had been so long pernicious to all the western parts of the kingdom.

The man who had been attacked was the guide, and care was taken to have a large number of bloodhounds with them, that no human means might be wanting towards their putting an entire end to these cruelties.

No sign of any habitation was to be found for a long time, and even when they came to the wretches' cave they took no notice of it, but were going to pursue their search along the seashore, the tide being then out. But some of the bloodhounds luckily entered this Cimmerian den, and instantly set up a most hideous barking, howling and yelping; so that the King, with his attendants, came back, and looked into it. They could not yet tell how to conceive that anything human could be concealed in a place where they saw nothing but darkness. Never the less, as the bloodhounds increased their noise, went farther in, and refused to come back again, they began to imagine there was some reason more than ordinary. Torches were now immediately sent for, and a great many men ventured in through the most intricate turnings and windings, till at last they arrived at that private recess from all the world, which was the habitation of these monsters.

Now the whole body, or as many of them as could, went in, and were all so shocked at what they beheld that they were almost ready to sink into the earth. Legs, arms, thighs, hands and feet of men, women and children were hung up in rows, like dried beef. A great many limbs lay in pickle, and a great mass of money, both gold and silver, with watches, rings, swords, pistols, and a large quantity of clothes, both linen and woollen, and an infinite number of other things, which they had taken from those whom they had murdered, were thrown together in heaps, or hung up against the sides of the den.

Sawney's family at this time, besides him, consisted of his wife, eight sons, six daughters, eighteen grandsons, and fourteen granddaughters, who were all begotten in incest.

These were all seized and pinioned by his Majesty's order in the first place; then they took what human flesh they found and buried it in the sands; afterwards loading themselves with the spoils which they found, they returned to Edinburgh with their prisoners, all the country, as they passed along, flocking to see this cursed tribe.

When they were come to their journey's end, the wretches were all committed to the Tolbooth, from whence they were the next day conducted under a strong guard to Leith, where they were all executed without any process, it being thought needless to try creatures who were even professed enemies to mankind. The men had their privy members cut off and thrown into the fire; their hands and legs were severed from their bodies; by which amputations they bled to death in some hours. The wife, daughters and grandchildren, having been made spectators of this just punishment inflicted on the men, were afterwards burnt to death in three several fires. They all in general died without the least signs of repentance; but continued, to the very last gasp of life cursing and venting the most dreadful imprecations upon all around, and upon all those who were instrumental in bringing them to such well merited punishments.[6]

What returns in the *Newgate Calendar* version—and which disappears again from some of the chapbook editions—is the opening assertion that the story is historically true, though this may have something to do with the calendar's moral context.

However, not all of the books lumped together as *Newgate Calendars* used the same story. In the 1825 edition of the *Terrific Register*, the Bean tale is more polished still, and subtly altered.

The Terrific Register

Sawney Beane was born in the county of East Lothian, about eight miles east of Edinburgh, in the reign of James VI. His father was a hedger and ditcher, and brought up his son in the same laborious employment. Naturally idle and vicious, he abandoned that place, along with a young woman equally idle and profligate, and they retired to the deserts of Galloway, and took up their habitation by the sea side. The place which Sawney and his wife selected for their dwelling, was a cave about a mile in length, and of considerable breadth; so near the sea that the tide often penetrated into the cave above two hundred yards. The entry had many intricate windings and turnings which led to the extremity of the subterraneous dwelling, which was literally 'the habitation of horrid cruelty.'

Sawney and his wife took shelter in this cave, and commenced their depredations. To prevent the possibility of detection, they murdered every person that they robbed. Destitute also of the means of obtaining any other food, they resolved to live upon human flesh. Accordingly, when they had murdered any man, woman, or child, they carried them to their den, quartered them, salted and pickled the members, and dried them for food. In this manner they lived, carrying on their depredations and murder, until they had eight sons and six daughters, eighteen grandsons, and fourteen grand-daughters, all the product of incest.

But, though they soon became numerous yet, such was the multitude who fell into their hands, that they had often superabundance of provisions, and would, at a distance from their own habitation, throw legs and arms of dried human bodies into the sea by night. These were often thrown out by the tide, and taken up by the country people, to the great consternation and dismay of all the surrounding inhabitants. Nor could any discover what had befallen the many friends, relations, and neighbours who had unfortunately fallen into the hands of these merciless cannibals.

In proportion as Sawney's family increased, every one that was able, acted his part in their horrid assassinations. They would attack four or six men on foot, but never more than two upon horseback. To prevent the possibility of escape, they would lay an ambush in every direction, that if they escaped those who first attacked, they might be assailed and renewed fury by another party, and inevitably murdered. By this means, they always secured their prey, and prevented detection.

At last, however, the vast number who were slain, had raised the inhabitants of the country, and all the woods and lurking places were carefully searched; and though they often passed by the mouth of the horrible den, it was never once suspected that any human being resided there. In this state of uncertainty and suspense, concerning the authors of such frequent massacres, several innocent travellers and inn-keepers were taken up upon suspicion; because, the persons who were missing, had been last seen in their company, or had last resided at their houses. The effect of this well-meant and severe justice, constrained the greater part of the inn-keepers in these parts, to abandon such employments, to the great inconvenience of those who travelled through that district.

Meanwhile, the country became depopulated, and the whole nation was surprised, how such numerous and unheard-of villainies and cruelties could be perpetrated, without the least discovery of the abominable actors. At length, Providence interposed in the following manner to terminate the horrid scene; one evening, a man and his wife were riding home upon the same horse from a fair which had been held in the neighbourhood; and being attacked, he made the most vigorous resistance: unfortunately, however, his wife was dragged from behind him, carried to a little distance, and her entrails instantly taken out. Struck with grief and horror, the husband continued to redouble his efforts to escape, and even trod some of them under his horse's feet. Fortunately for him, and for the inhabitants of that part of the country, in the meantime, twenty or thirty in a company came riding home from the same fair. Upon their approach, Sawney and his bloody crew fled into a thick wood, and hastened to their infernal den.

This man, who was the first that had ever escaped out of their hands, related to his neighbours what had happened, and shewed them the mangled body of his wife, which lay at a distance, the blood-thirsty wretches not having tie to carry it along with them. They were all struck with astonishment and horror, took him with them to Glasgow, and reported the whole adventure to the chief magistrate of the city. Upon this intelligence, he wrote to the king, informing him of the matter.

In a few days, his majesty in person, accompanied by four hundred men, went in quest of the perpetrators of such cruelties: the man who had his wife murdered before his eyes, went as their guide, with a

An illustration from the *Terrific Register* in 1825—'The Monster of Scotland, Sawney Bean'.

great number of blood-hounds, that no possible means might be left unattempted to discover the haunts of these execrable villains.

They searched the woods, traversed, and examined by the sea-shore; but though they passed by the entrance to their cave, they had no suspicion that any creature resided in that dark and dismal abode. Fortunately, however, some of the blood-hounds entered the cave, and raised up an uncommon barking and noise, indicating that they were about to seize their prey. The king and his men returned, but could scarcely conceive how any human being could reside in such a place of utter darkness, and where the entrance was difficult and narrow, but as the blood-hounds increased in their vociferation, and refused to return, it occurred to all that the cave ought to be explored to the extremity. Accordingly, a sufficient number of torches were provided. The hounds were permitted to pursue their course; a great number of men penetrated through all the intricacies of the path, and at length arrived at the private residence of these horrible cannibals.

They were followed by all the band, who were shocked to behold a sight unequalled in Scotland, if not in any part of the universe. Legs, arms, thighs, hands, and feet, of men, women, and children, were suspended in rows like dried beef. Some limbs and other members were soaked in pickle; while at great mass of money, both gold and silver, watches, rings, pistols, cloths, both woollen and linen, with an inconceivable quantity of other articles, were either thrown together in heaps, or suspended on the sides of the cave.

The whole cruel brutal family, to the number formally mentioned, were seized; the human flesh buried in the sand of the sea-shore: the immense booty carried away, and the king marched to Edinburgh with the prisoners. This new and wretched spectacle attracted the attention of the inhabitants, who flocked from all quarters to see this bloody and unnatural family as they passed along, which had increased, in the space of twenty-five years , to the number of twenty-seven men, and twenty-one women. Arrived in the capital, they were all confined in the Tolbooth, under a strong guard; they were next day conducted to the common place of execution in Leith Walk, and executed without any formal trial, it being deemed unnecessary to try those who were avowed enemies to all mankind, and of all social order.

The enormity of their crimes detected the severity of their death. The men had their privy-members thrown into the fire, their hands and legs were severed from their bodies, and they were permitted to bleed to death. The wretched mother of the whole crew, the daughter and grand-children, after being spectators of the death of the men, were caste into three separate fires and consumed to ashes. Nor did they, in general, display any signs of repentance or regret, but continued with their last breath, to pour forth the most dreadful curses and imprecations upon all around, and upon all those who were instrumental in bringing them to such well-merited punishment.[7]

Compared with the original by Captain Charles Johnson and the earlier *Newgate Calendar*, the authors of the *Terrific Register* have relied more on the chapbook editions of the Bean saga. Missing is the traditional introductory statement that this is a 'well attested' historical account—perhaps the editors realised that it was too farfetched for such a claim.

The changes to the story from the *Terrific Register* are subtle but noteworthy: where the Johnson version is situated in the reigns of James I and Queen Elizabeth, this version cites James VI. This is not the only edition to change the ruler who intervenes in the story, thus calling into question when the entire affair would actually have taken place, if at all. These discrepancies will be addressed in Chapter 11.

In the *Terrific Register*, only Sawney's father is employed as a ditcher and hedger, and—whilst it came to over a thousand in the previous version—

An image taken from the Captain Charles Johnson woodcut, printed in later chapbook and textbook editions. N. B. the addition of a kilt and tartan stockings to Sawney's dress.

the authors give no estimate of the number of victims. They probably felt that this statistic was a step too far and detracted from the authenticity of the tale: after all, gone too is the implausible assertion that the Beans never once visited any town or village for twenty-five years, the omission of which does lend the story more credibility.

Other missing elements include the spies sent into Galloway in search of the murderers, and t swords among the booty recovered in the Beans' cave—perhaps only referencing pistols was intended to modernise the tale.

The Morals of Sawney Bean

The *Newgate Calendar* series were suffused with allegorical teachings, and its treatment of the Bean story was no exception. While condemnation of murder hardly needs further clarification, other morals and aphorisms abound:

The condemnation of sloth: Sawney comes from a hardworking family, but choses to be idle.
Sawney falls in with a woman as vile and vicious as himself: alone, he would have been a murderer, but with this wife, he becomes a serial killer. This strongly resonates with the biblical narrative of Eve and the Fall.
Incest and its tangible connection with the family's pathological criminality, and vice versa.
The hole in Sawney's life where religion should be: he and his family shun civil society, and along with it the Church; they do not confess or repent their sins, but perish still cursing, implicitly dammed and destined for Hell.
Justice will be served: Sawney and his family's crimes are so horrific that the king himself is involved in their arrest and punishment; and they are not allowed to face trial, because they have renounced their humanity and their civil rights. Their crimes have consequences, and these consequences are proportionate to crimes themselves.
Beyond serial killing: cannibalism as an unnatural and unforgivable evil.
Perseverance: the unnamed man who manages to survive his encounter with the Beans does not give up when he is ambushed and forced to witness the slaughter of his wife.
Robbery and crime offer no reward: the Beans' cave is filled with the plunder of decades of killing, but they live in animal-like squalor. For all of their riches, in many ways they lead a wretched and impoverished form of existence. Crime isolates, and does not pay.

Fear and the rush to judgement: the Galwegians' fear led them to falsely accuse and hang innocent innkeepers.

The story of Sawney Bean could easily be converted into a set of lessons for readers—but this would not have suited the readership or the zeitgeist surrounding the *Newgate Calendars*.

John Nicolson's Version

While the *Newgate Calendars* gave credibility and weight to the story of Sawney Bean, it was author John Nicholson who firmly replanted the tale in both Scottish history and folklore. Nicholson's version is one of the most often cited, yet by the time he wrote *Historical and Traditional Tales in Prose and Verse, Connected With The South of Scotland* in 1843, he was simply making editorial adjustments to the Bean stories already in print. At the time, few books discussed Scottish history or traditions, let alone Galloway's, but Nicholson adopted a story perpetuated by the English for a semi-officially Scottish tale. The complete text of the Nicholson version is provided in Appendix E.

According to Nicholson, the throne was occupied by James I of Scotland at the time of the crimes, and he makes no reference to Queen Elizabeth. He does replicate the introductory paragraph so common to earlier editions—claiming that the story was a 'historical fact'—and it is clear that Nicholson used the J. Ferraby chapbook, or one similar to it, as the basis for his story—many sections are taken word-for-word from this chapbook.

The Victorian readership for which Nicholson published his book accounts for most of the small alterations that he does contribute, namely his removal of some of the more grotesque imagery—such as the female cannibals sucking the blood of the ambushed wife as though it were wine. Likewise, Nicholson removes allusions to the captured men's privy members being cut off, favouring instead the simple amputation of hands and legs.

What mattered most was the reconfiguration of this tantalizing horror story into the domain of Scottish history; however unsubstantiated, it had gone from a peddled chapbook to propounded historical episode in just two generations. Nevertheless, Sawney Bean soon made an embellished come back to fiction.

5

Fictionalizing Sawney Bean

Keeping only to the best of such productions it is indeed an astonishing gallery that we have—Thrawn Janet; Tod Lapraik, 'the commonplace weaver wi' the kind o' holy smile, a muckle fat white hash o' a man like creish, set in bright sunny daylight, among the seafowl'; Sawney Bean, the Galloway cannibal; Burke and Hare, the Edinburgh corpse-providers, to turn from literature to real life; and, one of the best of the lot....[1]

Sawney Bean, the Play

In 1798, the story of Sawney Bean was still being circulated in only a handful of prints, most of them chapbooks. It became the subject of the play *Songs Duets and Choruses in the Semi-Comic Pantomime of Harlequinn Highlander, or Sawney Bean's Cave*, performed at the Jones Royal Circus in London; but, from what evidence can be found, the play only showed eleven times.[2]

The play itself is about a young man who is attacked by Sawney Bean and his family. Their would-be victim is initially tempted to join the 'robbers of the glen', knowing that refusing to would mean death … or worse, but he eventually escapes from their clutches. The story is only thinly detailed: for instance, we know only that the Beans are highwaymen—cannibalism is only ever hinted at. This alone signals an assumption that the viewers were already familiar with the tale.

While hardly a stunning success, it does mark the newfound potential of the Beans for song and stage. It opened their story to a wider audience, and demonstrated how such a bit of historical fiction could be more widely adapted for entertainment. The framework of the Bean tale seems to possess a timeless quality that invited new interpretation, such as in the writing of *The Grey Man*.

The Grey Man

While the tale of Sawney Bean had been absorbed into Galwegian folklore, the story gained more notoriety than ever in the form of a novel. In 1896, Samuel Rutherford Crockett's *The Grey Man* transformed Sawney Bean from one-dimensional antagonist to fully formed character.

Crockett made his living novelizing tales of the lowland Scots, particularly those of Galloway. He had been born in 1850 in Kirkcudbrightshire, and his stories often reflect an intimate knowledge of the people, the land, and the customs. It is clear that he had long been exposed to the Bean legend when he incorporated it into *The Grey Man*. A respected novelist, Crockett cultivated a close friendship with Robert Lewis Stevenson, a contemporary and peer. He wrote over twenty novels, all intertwined with the Scots among which he had been raised.

The Grey Man is set just prior to the reign of James VI of Scotland and I of England. It is a tale similar to Dumas's *Three Musketeers* in terms of swashbuckling fights and adventures, and revolves around a feud between the Cassillis and Bargany branches of the Kennedy family. The protagonist, Launcelot Kennedy, runs headlong into an endless series of battles and fights across the Galloway landscape, and falls in love with Nell Kennedy.

An illustration of Sawney Bean and his family in Crockett's *The Grey Man*.

There are two antagonists in *The Grey Man*: one is John Mure of Auchindrayne, the Grey Man himself; the other is none other than the legendary cannibal, Sawney Bean. Although the Beans only feature as a horrific subplot of the journeys and battles of Launcelot Kennedy, Victorian reviewers were still critical of this graphic aspect of the book.

> The hideous shore cannibals, to whom we are introduced, are too repulsive and unnatural. We wish Mr. Crockett had kept them out of his book, but he has a strange liking for such things, and these monstrosities certainly add a touch of horror that some people claim in a story. The books is full of blood, but it is in its way a real masterpiece.[3]

Samuel Crockett favoured spelling Sawney 'Sawny'—since much of the dialogue is written with local accents, this change was most likely meant to deemphasise the 'nee' at the end of the name.

References to Sawney are many in the novel, and are almost always laced with dread:

> He told me that he had heard what as a-doing—how that the Mures and the Drummurchies, together with Sawny Bean, the save carl that was called of the common people, 'The Earl of Hell,' had gotten into Laird of Culzean in a little summer house in a walled garden and were there worrying him to death.[4]

The impetus for Launcelot to interact with the Beans is that the treasure of Kelwood was being kept in their cave. For the first time in written form, the location of the cave where Sawney and his family took refuge—'on the seashore of Bennanbrack, over against the hill of Benerard'[5]— is revealed, albeit in fictional form.

> The neighbourhood of the Beanae was well known to all that trafficked about the town of Girvan. It was a dangerous and ill-famed place, and many innocent people had very mysteriously lost their lives there, or at least disappeared to the return no more.[6]

One character describes the region near the Beans' cave in the story as treacherous.

> 'They are no that ill in this pairt o' the country. They wad only hae killed ye,' she said, is if it would have been a satisfaction to us. 'It is doon aboot the Benane that the real ill folk abide.'[7]

In his travels, Launcelot Kennedy makes enquiries about the Benane region where the cave is alleged to be.

> 'Good wif,' said I, 'we are thinking of going by Ballantrae to the town of Stranrawer. The direct way, I hear, is by the Benane. What think ye—is the road a good one?'
> 'Ye are a sonsy lad,' she said, 'ye wad mak' braw pickin' for the teeth o' Sawny Bean's bairns. They wad roast your ribs fresh and fresh till they were done. Syne they would pickle your quarters for winter. The line o' you wad be as guid as a Christmas mart to them.'
> 'Hoot, good wife,' said I, 'ye ken that a' this talk aboot Sawny Bean's folk is juist blethers—made to fright bairns frae gallivanting at night.'
> 'Ye'll maybe get news o' that gin Sawny puts his knife intil your throat. Ye hae heard o' my man. James Bannatyne is not a man easily feared, but not for the Earldom o' Cassillis wad he gang that shore road to Ballantrae his lane.'[8]

Crockett seamlessly integrates the legend of the Beans into his own fictional narrative.

> The next moment mighty fear took hold on me. All that I had heard since my childhood, about the unknown being who dwelled upon the shoreside of Benane and lived no man knew how, ran through my mind—his monstrous form, his cloven feet that made steads on the ground like those of a beast, his huge hairy arms, clawed at the finger ends like the toes of a bear. I minded me of the fireside tales of travellers who had lost their way in that fastness, and who, falling into the power of this savage tribe, returned no more to kindlier places. I minded also how none might speak to the prowler by night, no get answer from him—how every expedition against him had come to naught, because that he was protected by a power stronger than himself, warned and advised by an intelligence higher than his own. Besides none had been able to find the abode, nor yet to enter into the secret defenses where lurked the man-beast of Benerard.[9]

Crockett elaborates a more detailed description of the cavern:

> After that I went ranging higher and thither among all the passages and twinings of the cave, yet never daring to go very far from the place where we were, lest I should not be able to find my way back. For it was an ill, murderous, uncanny abode, where every step that I took something strange swept across my face of slithered clammily along my cheek, making me grue too my very boon marrows.[10]

An extract detailing Young Launcelot Kennedy's final expedition into the home of Sawney and his clan can be found in Appendix F. The saga ends with the rescue of Launcelot Kennedy by the king's party; Sawney battles with one of his friends and in the end is stabbed to death; and the Grey Man is apprehended and forced to reckon with the king's justice.

Characterisation in Crockett

It is worth noting that Crockett's portrayal of Sawney is somewhere between human and animal. He likens Sawney's relationship with his family to the dominance of a wolf over a pack: the members of his murderous tribe are barely clad, naked, and filthy; bucktoothed and cruel, Sawney barely speaks, but instead growls; he has no regard at all for humans, yet despite his brutality, enjoys fierce loyalty from his family. Yet Sawney's infamous reputation supersedes the character himself; fear of Sawney and his treatment of victims is so great, that one of the characters would prefer to be killed by Launcelot rather than risk capture by the Beans.

Crockett utilises all of the props already common to the story—arms and legs hanging blackened on the wall awaiting consumption, for instance. The treasure that the family has amassed, including that of Kelwood, is—again—not used to relieve the Beans' squalor.

Crockett provides us with our first comprehensive insight into the Beans' cave, and the rituals and routines of their daily lives there. The author depicts strong links to hell and the supernatural—not far from Shakespeare's description of witches and their behaviours—in which Sawney appears immune to physical danger. He is a creature, not a man, yet is possessed of a cunning that has allowed him and his family to survive all this time.

The West Port Murderers

Reality caught up with the Bean saga when a string of killings perpetrated in Edinburgh by William Burke and William Hare came to light, later known as 'the West Port Murders'.

Serial killing was not unheard of in Britain before the nineteenth century, but its news had never been so rapidly and widely disseminated, and real-life examples had therefore seemed few and far. In this sense, the West Port Murders represented a turning point, and can be accredited with adding validity to the tale of the Beans.

Scotland's first real and fully documented serial killers, Burke and Hare, were an unlikely pair of Irish immigrants. Burke had moved to Scotland

Above left: William Hare.

Above right: William Burke.

Left: Doctor Knox.

in 1817 and had a variety of odd jobs; he lived with his mistress, Helen McDougal. Hare had married the widow Margaret Laird, who ran a lodging house and whom he had met in 1828: they lived in Tanner's Close, Margaret's house.

A tenant at Tanner's Close—an old army pensioner—passed away, leaving Margaret with overdue rent. At the time, medical schools paid handsome sums for bodies needed for training purposes, which had given rise to a new, illegal business—grave robbing. This was a filthy and labour-intensive profession, one fraught with risk of being apprehended. Burke and Hare, however, did not have to undertake such arduous labour—they had the corpse of the dead tenant. They filled the coffin of the man with heavy sacks and took the body to a professor of anatomy at Edinburgh University, Dr Robert Knox. The doctor was well known in Edinburgh as a skilled army surgeon at the Battle of Waterloo. He paid Burke and Hare £7 10s 0d—more than enough to make up for the £4 worth of rent that the deceased owed—which left them with a tidy profit.

Another lodger, named Joseph, at Tanner's Close fell ill, and Burke and Hare felt that he would make another fine specimen for Dr Knox; however, Joseph clung to life much longer than the two had hoped. Rather than wait for Joseph to die, they decided to speed up the process, and smothered him. After another visit to Dr Knox, Burke and Hare once more pocketed a sizeable reward: they had gone from selling dead bodies to becoming murderers. But sick lodgers were an unreliable source of income. The pair determined that, rather than wait for the next opportunity, they would create it themselves.

Burke and Hare's next victim was Abigail Simpson, an elderly woman, whom they plied her with alcohol, and took back to Tanner's Close. She was given drinks to the point of losing consciousness, upon which they smothered her. That night, they carried her body to Dr Knox, who allegedly made a passing comment on the freshness of the corpse her—but paid nevertheless.

Again making alcohol as their modus operandi, the pair next supplied Dr Knox with the body of a prostitute named Mary Haldane. They then became more brazen, attempting to kill two women at once—Mary Patterson and Janet Brown. Mary was easily driven into a stupor, and met the same fate as their previous victims, but Janet proved to be more than capable of holding her liquor, and left.

Up until Mary's death, Burke and Hare had been targeting the unseen society of Edinburgh—people who held no status, and would not be missed. But Mary was attractive, and well known in the city. Dr Knox was even concerned that one of his medical students might recognise her body when it was laid out for dissection.

The duo murdered several others, including Mary Haldane's daughter, who fell into the same trap as her mother. One victim, Effie, was even known to Burke—she made her living scavenging for leather scraps which she sold to him in his daytime capacity as a cobbler. The pair were paid £10 for her body. In one scenario, Burke 'saved' an inebriated woman from arrest, instead escorting her back to her lodgings and killing her there. Burke was supposedly the more aggressive and vicious of the two men.

One pair of victims was an elderly woman and her twelve-year-old deaf and mute grandson. Burke overdosed the woman with her painkillers, while Hare, fearing that the deaf-mute might trace the crime back to them, stretched him over his knee and proceeded to break his back. These victims were likewise sold to Dr Knox, who asked no questions, but must have known what had occurred.

The duo had a falling out of sorts, because Hare killed at least one victim on his own and failed to include Burke in the transaction with Dr Knox. Burke and his girlfriend moved out of the building they shared with the Hares, which seemed to calm the situation. While their significant others did not take part in the killings, they possessed at least tacit knowledge of how the men were earning money. One of their victims was Anne MacDougal, a cousin of Helen's from Falkirk, which may indicate that the latter was willing to contribute her own relatives to Burke's fare.

Burke and Hare both became sloppy near the end. One of their last victims, eighteen-year-old James Wilson—affectionately known as 'Daft Jamie'—was a pleasant, mentally impaired man well known to the streets of Edinburgh. Jamie fought back and it took both of the men to finally kill him. When Jamie was declared missing, his disappearance was noticed by many in Edinburgh, and one of Knox's students recognised his body on the operating table. Usually after a murder, Burke would dispose of the victim's clothing in the Union Canal, but in this case gave the victim's clothes to his nephews—directly incriminating himself with physical evidence.

Burke and Hare's final victim proved to be their undoing. Mrs. Mary Docherty was lured to the lodging house under the pretence that she and Burke were related. When they arrived, there were two other guests present—James and Ann Gray—so Mrs. Docherty could not immediately be dispatched. When the Grays left for the night, the neighbours allegedly heard the sounds of a struggle and a woman's voice calling out 'murder!', but did nothing.

The next day, the Grays returned because Ann wanted to look for a pair of stockings that she had inadvertently left behind the night before. Burke became agitated and would not let her look under the bed where she knew she had left them. When Burke and Hare left in the early evening, the Grays checked under the bed and found the body of Mrs. Docherty covered in straw. Helen McDougal who offered them a bribe of 10 pounds a week for their silence, but they rejected the proposition and contacted the police.

By the time the police arrived, the body had been removed. While being questioned, Burke claimed that Docherty had left at 7 a.m., while McDougal claimed that she had left the night before. Their inconsistency was enough to warrant their arrest, and an anonymous tip led the police to Knox's dissecting tables, where they found Mrs. Docherty's fresh corpse. Mr. and Mrs. Hare were immediately arrested as well, bringing an end to their ten-month killing spree, of which sixteen victims are known.[11]

Hare and his wife agreed to turn King's evidence in return for immunity, leaving Burke to bear the brunt of the blame. The trial received press coverage all over Britain, fuelled by the grisly details of the crimes—the *Edinburgh Evening Courant* alone sold 8,000 copies during the trail.

Burke was hung on 28 January 1829 in front of over 20,000 spectators. His body was dissected in public at Edinburgh University's Old College, and his skeleton displayed at the University of Edinburgh's Anatomy Museum. Burke and Hare's death masks were cast in plaster, and are on display in the Surgeons' Hall. Burke's skin was taken by souvenir-hunters, and a calling card case made from his skin is displayed at The Police Information Centre in Edinburgh's Royal Mile.

Hare was released in February 1829, and tried to flee to Dumfries in Galloway. He had been spotted on the train by a juror-counsel for one of the victims, who happened to be on the same train. Word was wired ahead and by the time Hare arrived in Dumfries, he was greeted by 8,000 angry protestors. Hare managed to flee to England, and is alleged to have died blind and a pauper in London.

Dr Knox was hounded by angry mobs, who broke his windows and burned him in effigy. He eventually fled Edinburgh out of fear for his life, but continued to teach medicine until he died in 1862.

The influence of the Burke and Hare affair on public perceptions of serial killing can hardly be overemphasised. They are even commemorated in the popular Edinburgh nursery rhyme:

> Up the close and doun the stair,
> But and ben wi' Burke and Hare.
> Burke's the butcher, Hare's the thief,
> Knox the boy that buys the beef.

The influence of these killers on society is so great that the term 'burking' has since been added to the dictionary (meaning to suffocate or smother for purposes of dissection).

The execution scene of William Burke.

In the aftermath of the notorious Burke and Hare, the people of Scotland found the tale of Sawney Bean much more plausible. Locals could now point to Burke and Hare as testimony that such tales were anchored in reality.

Meanwhile, Crockett's novel, *The Grey Man*, carved out a lasting legacy for the Beans: it tied the Beans to an actual physical location, exactly situating their cave, and temporally pinned down the story to the reign of James I/VI. In narrowing the field down to one locality, was Crockett acting on the reports of Galwegians or the product of his imagination?

Part Two

LOCATING THE HISTORY

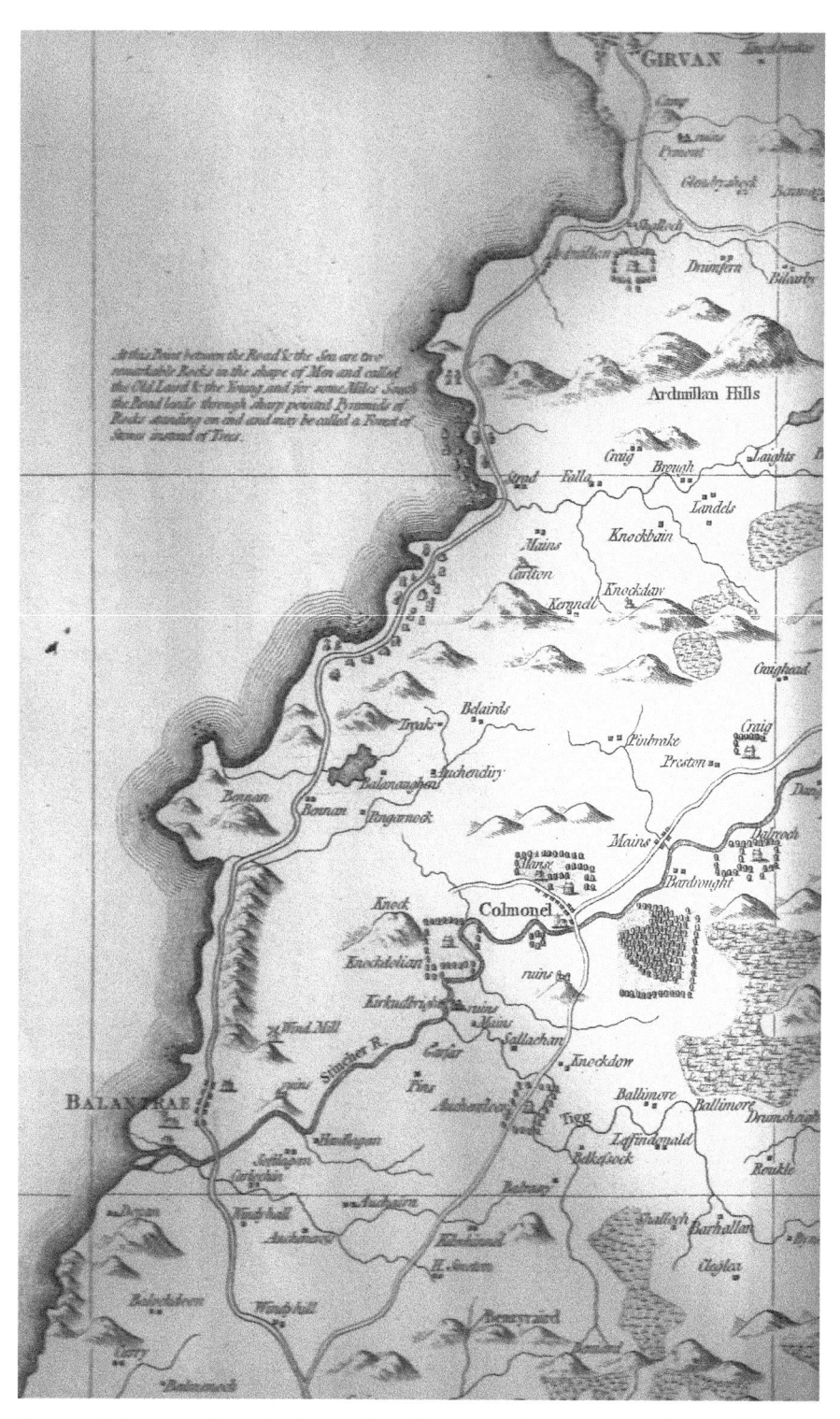

A map of the area where the Beans allegedly operated in 1775. (*Author's collection*)

6

Which King James?

Sawney Bean: Said to have been a native of East Lothian who settled in a cave at Bennane Head, near Ballantrae, in the reign of James I (or perhaps James VI) and lived by robbery, murder and cannibalism.[1]

The King Sets the Stage

Any attempt to authenticate the tale of the Beans requires some sort of temporal reference, hence the naming of a king in every Bean account. Indeed, since Captain Charles Johnson first made the reference, the naming of the Scottish sovereign has become an integral part of the story.

> Sawney Beane was born in the County of East Lothian, about eight or nine Miles eastward of the City of Edinburgh, some Time in the Reign of Queen Elizabeth, whilst King James I. govern'd only in Scotland.[2]

The chapbook editions of the Aldermary Church, J. Ferraby, and F. Jollie and Sons all either mimic or resemble this. John Nicholson, however, break the pattern with 'the reign of James I. of Scotland'.[3]

How deliberate was Nicholson's omission of Queen Elizabeth from the opening lines? And which James I was he referring to—King James I of Scotland or James I of England (and IV of Scotland)? Some books take wild guesses at the dates, estimating them at between 1360 and 1370—a period that significantly predates the reign of either candidate.[4]

King James I of Scots

James I of Scotland reigned between 4 April 1406 and 21 February 1437. Like many rulers of that period, his reign was marked with brutality and

King James I of Scotland.

bloodshed. James was the youngest of three sons of the Stuart King Robert III. By the time he was eight years old, his two older brothers had died—one under dubious circumstances at the hand of his uncle. James was raised in an era where the throne was constantly threatened from all sides, usually by other family members. During one clash with nobles, the prince was forced to take refuge on the Bass Rock in the Firth of Forth. When he fled to France, his ship was overtaken by pirates, and he was delivered as a prisoner to Henry IV of England. Only a few days after being put in captivity, his father, Robert III, died. This left the heir to the Scottish crown, at the age of twelve, in the hands of the English monarch—James would remain in English captivity for eighteen years.

James was educated at the English court, and went on to fight the French for England in 1420-1421. King Henry V had even used James to lead troops against Scottish forces who were fighting for the French, and after the siege of Melun, James oversaw the hanging of a number of Scots who had battled against him on the field. He was knighted for his service, and after Henry V died in France, he returned his body to England. Henry's son, Henry VI, was little more than an infant, so power fell to a ruling council.

The ruling council was inclined to release James under the terms of a ransom, and the Scottish noble Archibald Earl of Douglas allied himself with James in order to cement his own position of power. Under pressure from Douglas, the temporary ruler of Scotland, Murdoch Stewart, who had been held captive with James for a short time, finally backed his return.

The Douglases hailed from Galloway, where they had risen to power when the MacDougals had fallen from it; in the early fifteenth century, they were one of the most influential families in Scotland, known even as kingmakers. The Douglases led a contingent of 10,000 men from all over Scotland to France to fight the English in 1423. The Earl of Douglas carried a wide range of titles, including The Earl of Wigton, Lord of Galloway, Lord of Bothwell, Lord of Annandale, Lord of Eskdale, Lord of Longueville, Duke of Touraine, and Marshal of France. Most historians claim, rightfully so, that the Douglas clan was nearly as powerful as the Scottish royal family.

James I's ransom was a hefty one, which required taxing the Scots for the return of their rightful ruler. This—combined with the fact that James had fought against Scotsmen in France—did not benefit his appeal to the Scottish people. In many respects, James was a foreigner: in spite of being born in Scotland, he had received an English education, had strong sympathies with England, and had married Joan Beaufort, a cousin of Henry VI.

When he was crowned King James I at the age of thirty in 1424, he assumed the rule of a land in dire economic straits. James undertook reforms of land holdings to restore financial stability; founded the Scottish Court of Session; sought to remodel the Scottish Parliament along English lines; and increased his own military strength, much to the dislike of nobles (with standing troops of their own).

James I's personality did not help his cause. He was known for his quick temper and ruthlessness when dealing with his enemies. In the second year of his reign, he called a session of parliament at Perth where he executed four opposing nobles, and seized their lands. Two years later, he called the Highland chiefs to Inverness under the pretence of peaceful negotiation, but killed three of them and imprisoned more than forty others. He upset the often delicate balance of power in Scotland by restoring the prestige of the Scottish monarchy, while at the same time he lashing out at foes such as the Dukes of Albany, whose lands he forfeited. He arrested the old Earl of Lennox and Sir Robert Graham of the Kincardine family—the man who would one day end his reign.[5] One of the only nobles to evade the fiery temper of the king was the Earl of Douglas, in recognition of the power that his family wielded. And James was still significantly indebted to England, as part of his terms of ransom, but he simply ignored the debt. This default left nobles to languish in English captivity, which further eroded his opponents' power, but simultaneously fanned the flames of dissent among others— hardly actions conducive to stabilizing the economy. Instead, James spent large sums of money on the Linlithgow Palace.

James had stripped the Earl of Strathearn of his title and sent him to England as a hostage for the debt that he owed. This was too much for the Earl's uncle, Robert Graham, who managed to beat a retreat from James reach into the highlands, aided by the Earl of Atholl. Graham organised a party and raided the monastery of the Blackfriars in Perth, where James was in attendance. Graham and his men butchered James, and were in turn tortured and killed by the order of the Queen, Joan Beaufort.[6] The reign of James passed to his seven-year-old son, James II.

So was King James I the ruler of Scotland when the crimes of Sawney Bean supposedly took place? There are no records in the National Archives of Scotland of James I mounting a military expedition into Galloway in search of a killer. In fact, given the iron grip of his allies—the Douglas clan—over the region, such an expedition would have been pointless. The Earl of Douglas was more than capable, and sufficiently armed, to mount his own manhunt, and having James march an army through his heartland would have been interpreted either as a sign of weakness or an outright threat from the king.

Nicholson's claim lacks any kind of documentation or logic. We must therefore turn our attention towards King James VI of Scotland and I of England.

King James VI of Scotland and I of England

James VI of Scotland and I of England and Ireland ruled from 24 July 1567 to 27 March 1625. He had the distinction of being the only son of Mary Queen of Scots, born on 19 June 1566. Mary's reign was marked with

King James VI of Scotland and I of England.

religious strife and political insecurity, and James's father, Lord Darnley, was murdered in early 1567 in an unexplained explosion. In May, Mary married James Hepburn, the Forth Earl of Bothwell, a man suspected of killing her former husband and James's father. Mary had been suspected of having an affair for some time with the Earl, who, as a Protestant, had only recently divorced his first wife. Mary's marriage to the Earl especially upset her Catholic supporters, who did not recognise the Earl's divorce, while Protestants were stilled shocked that Mary might even consider marrying a man implicated in the death of her husband. Yet Mary seemed almost aloof to this controversy, believing she had consolidated a tighter control over the nobles than she really had.

In June of 1567, a band of Protestant rebels arrested Mary and imprisoned her in Loch Leven Castle. She was forced to flee to England, where she was placed under protective custody, and forced to abdicate and cede the throne to her infant son James that same year.

DÆMONOLOGIE,
IN FORME
OF A DIA-
LOGVE,

Diuided into three books:

WRITTEN BY THE HIGH
and mightie Prince, IAMES by the
grace of God King of England,
Scotland, France *and* Ireland,
Defender of the Faith, &c.

LONDON,
Printed by *Arnold Hatfield* for
Robert Wald-graue.
1603

The *Daemonologie*, by King James VI.

James was raised by regents as James VI of Scotland, and was well read and educated. He was held hostage for several months by a group of Protestant earls, and upon his liberation in June of 1583 determined to assert greater control over Scotland. He maintained strong ties with England, and strengthened the relations of the two governments by signing the Treaty of Berwick. Whereas his mother had failed to win Queen Elizabeth's favour, James VI pledged to support her during the crisis of the Spanish Armada.

Young James became intrigued with the concept of witchcraft after a trip to Denmark, where witch-hunting and trials were rising into popularity. James believed strongly in the power of witches, and even wrote a book on the perils of witchcraft, the *Daemonologie*. Scotland already had a law concerning witchcraft in place—the Witchcraft Act of 1563—but it was not until James VI's rule that it was executed with vigour.

James was so fascinated by the black arts that he attended the North Berwick Witch Trials in 1590. One of the accused, Agnes Sampson, was examined personally by James at Holyrood Palace. Sampson was strapped to the wall of her cell by 'a witch's bridle', an iron instrument with four sharp prongs forced into the mouth, so that two prongs pressed against her tongue, and the two others against her cheeks. Agnes was subjected to sleep deprivation and torture, and confessed to the fifty-three indictments against her. She was ultimately strangled and then burned as a witch.

James VI ruled solely over Scotland until 1603. On the day that Queen Elizabeth I—the last of Henry VIII's descendants—died without an heir, he was named King, and was formally crowned James I of England and Ireland on 25 July 1603. He assumed the English throne under the premise that he would return to Scotland every three years—a promise he failed to keep.

Yet James saw himself as the embodiment of Union. Not all nobles agreed, and he faced several plots to depose him within a year of ascending the English throne: the Bye Plot, wherein a group of Roman Catholics planned to kidnapping him, for one (James responded by expelling all Roman Catholic clergy from the realm); the Main Plot, spawned by a group of nobles who sought to replace him with his cousin Arabella Stuart—among those imprisoned for colluding in this plot was Sir Walter Raleigh.

In 1605, perhaps the most devious and well-known plan to assassinate James VI and I was foiled. A group of English Catholics secretly moved thirty-six barrels of gunpowder into a crawl space beneath Parliament, with the intention of blowing it up when the king, and his family, would be attending the opening on 5 November. The Gunpowder Plot was exposed when Guy Fawkes, one of the perpetrators, was captured and the explosives uncovered.

King James VI and I ruled Scotland 'with the pen'.[7] He became more and more distanced from Scotland as the years past, preferring to remain in England. Matters were not helped by his persecution of Catholics, which lasted over a decade, for since the Covenanter Movement, the Scots had retained a strong penchant for religious rebellion, and the crown's attempts to impose religious order were often met with an armed response.

The last years of James's life were spent in pain. At the age of fifty he contracted arthritis, gout, and kidney stones. He began to drink heavily and lost all of his teeth, and on 27 March 1625—during a bout of dysentery—James died, passing on the throne to his second son Charles.

King James VI and I was one of the most documented rulers of Scotland and England in terms of archival material, but a comprehensive search through the National Archives of Scotland does not reveal any reference to a military mission across Galloway in search of a serial killer. In fact, his rule did not see a single large-scale military incursion into Scotland.

A visit to Galloway would have been sensational news, and as such would have been circulated in the local and national press, for instance like his 1587 visit to the royal castle in Kirkcudbright—on this occasion, even his minor activities were recorded, including the presentation of a silver gun to local chieftains.[8] It is therefore unlikely that the king pursuing a man-eating, serial-killing family would have gone un-noted.

Yet King James VI and I remains the likeliest candidate for the earliest accounts, when 'the Reign of Queen Elizabeth, whilst King James I. govern'd only in Scotland,' given that he was the only monarch to rule Scotland while Elizabeth sat on the English throne.

Of Witchcraft

King James's near obsession with witchcraft and witch trials—which almost always ended in the same fiery fate as the Bean family—might better explain his role in the legend. It is therefore reasonable to suggest that a reference to James VI and I's reign was meant to create an association between the acts of the Beans and the witchcraft trials that were prevalent at the time.

Claims of witchcraft were hardly new to Galloway when James was crowned King—all he did was increase its public profile and organise communities against it. Given the strong religious ties people of Galloway had, finding and killing witches was always likely to become a popular activity. Between the Protestant Reformation in 1559 and the Union of Parliaments in 1707, it is estimated that over 3,000 witches were executed in Scotland.[9]

The Malt Cross, the site of witch executions in Ayr. (*Carnegie Library, Ayr*)

THE OLD MALT CROSS.

Many of these prosecutions and executions were highly documented, yet in none of the records or books relating to the witch trials of this period—such as the *Hereditary Sheriffs of Galloway*, or *Historical Tales and Legends of Ayrshire*—do Sawney Bean and his clan make an appearance.[10]

It was surprisingly easy to be accused of witchcraft. All it took in some cases was a cow not producing milk after someone walked past it, or talking to oneself. It was not uncommon for gypsies and tramps wandering through a town to attract the label and be killed. Margaret Wallace was executed for witchcraft in 1629 after suffering a 'brain fever' that left her mentally damaged and caused the Reverend William Adair to associate her with the devil. She was burned at the Malt Cross in the middle of Ayr, never confessed, and was said to have died while praying. Her remains were buried in the churchyard of St. Johns in Ayr.[11]

Margaret Wallace is often connected with the folklore concerning another local witch, Maggie Osborne. Local legend has it that Witch Osborn was accused of being trained in the black arts by Lord Fail. She ran a public house (inn) in Ayr for nearly fifty years, and was said to pray to her charms and fly across Galloway at night, 'bewitching cattle, turning ale sour, 'charming', wives and maidens, and generally misconducting herself.'[12] One night, she came across a funeral procession, and to avoid being caught, she turned herself into a beetle and hid in a horse hoof print. A man stepped on her, nearly killing her, and Maggie swore revenge. Her spell forced him to forget to say grace over dinner, allowing her to bury his home in snow. The weight of the snow was so great it broke the roof and killed him, his wife, and seven of his children. One son who was at sea was spared, so Maggie stirring up a storm to kill him. Such was the vindictiveness of Maggie Osborne. In the morning, she was incapacitated, allowing local officials to arrest her for witchcraft. She too is presumed to have met her fate on the Maltese Cross in Ayr, burned at the stake.[13]

While the tale of Maggie Osborne is mostly a piece of fiction, Margaret Wallace's trial is well documented. The Maltese or Malt Cross in Ayr became the regional method for the execution of witches. Poised as it was at a crossroads in the heart of Ayr, the bodies were often put on display for long periods of time, and the executions witnessed by many.

In Dumfries alone from 1657 to 1659, there was a brief period where nine women were executed for practicing witchcraft. The nine women were ordered by the High Court of the Judiciary to first be first strangled, then burned on Sunday 13 April 1659. They were taken down along the riverbank on the Whitesands and executed all together—this was one of the largest witch executions of the age.[14] The punishment meted out to convicted witches was savage:

> It is recorded that His Majesty, in the celebrated case of Dr Fian, charged with sorcery in 1591, devised for the benefit of the accused, 'a most straunge torment,' to wit: all his ten finger-nails were 'riven' or pulled off, 'and under everie nayle there was thrust in two needels over, even up to their heads'; further, the patient's legs were shockingly smashed in the boots, 'whereby they were made unserviceable forever.' Again in 1601, Archibald Cornwall, an Edinburgh town officer, having in the course of

his duty exposed for sale by public 'roup' or auction at the Market Cross certain 'poinded gear' (sequestered effects), which including a picture of the King, he, with unconscious humour, did hang the same upon a nail in the adjacent gibbet, then unoccupied in order that intending purchasers might the better view the Royal features. James waxed exceeding wroth. He directed that that unhappy officer be forthwith hanged in place of the portrait for the space of twenty-four hours, with a ticket affixed to his forehead descriptive of the enormity of his crime, and that thereafter the gibbet, as art and part of the offence, should be committed to the flames.[16]

If the tale of the Beans were true, it would have taken place 1567 and 1625—while Elizabeth was Queen of England. The window of time for these crimes can be further narrowed down to between 1567 and 1603, with an emphasis on the later years, when James was old enough to have undertaken a military expedition into Galloway.

While this much can be surmised, there is no tangible evidence to support James VI and I's association with the Beans or their execution. While the method of the latter is consistent with the torture of witches promoted by James, this alone is not evidence enough.

7

The Cimmerian Den

Epicureans who want to know more about the Galloway cannibal, Sawney Bean, should be directed to the cave south of Bennane Head.... There is, of course, no 'real' Sawney Bean cave, so this one will do just as well as another. Sawney Bean barbecues should be held on the shore.[1]

The Home and Butcher's Shop

The site of the Beans' den is first given written mention in *The Grey Man*, and seems to root the story to in reality. This is the only book to assign the Beans a precise location, '… on the seashore of Bennanbrack, over against the hill of Benerard'.[2] It faces the sea, at Bennane Head on the Ayrshire coast.

Earlier written accounts of the Bean saga never did the same. Given that Crockett's work is fictional, was he using a local's knowledge of the legends to fill in a much overlooked gap in the tale? Or was he simply using an identifiable cave to better anchor his story?

Two Possible Dens of Evil

There are two potential caves in the area of Bennane Head—between Girvan and Ballantrae—which have been associated with the Beans.

The first of these, Bennane Cave, has gone by several names over the years (still the case today). Its most common name is 'Snib's Cave', in reference to Snibb Scott, a colourful tramp who lived there until his death in 1983. It is located north of Ballantrae and in proximity to Bennane Head. At present, this cave is walled shut with a doorway to block entrance, and locals have erected a small memorial to Snib Scott opposite of the cave,[3] who died of hypothermia—despite hospitalisation—upon discovery in the

Bennane Head on a 1940s postcard. (*Author's collection*)

cave.[4] However, this cave is accessible at all times, regardless of the tide, so does not fit the description of the Bean cave exactly.

The second cave site is the one most commonly associated with Bennane Head. It lies further north, on the coast near the bay of Balcreuchan Port, and is largely considered to be the one, if it ever existed, that the Beans made their home. It is not easily accessible, if at all, during high tide—though the tide does not enter the cavern as far as two hundred yards—and the rocky point rises over two hundred feet above the sea. In the 1930s, the Ordnance Survey Maps for the area identified this as 'Sawney Beane's Cave', and still do today; however, local historians claim this was an error.[5]

Even *The Queen's Scotland* guide lists this site as the cave in question.

> Northward from Ballantrae the road to Girvan and Ayr runs magnificently along the edge of the sea. Some three miles from Ballentrae it rounds Bennane Head and gives us exhilarating views of Ailsa Craig, the Isle of Arran, and the regal Firth of Clyde. Slightly north of the headland and at the food of the cliffs is a tidal cave reputed to have been the lair of the cannibal, Sawney Bean, about whom we can read in Crockett's *The Grey Man*.[6]

The cave itself has been marked out on maps for several centuries, though most local historians state that it was used by smugglers, gypsies, or tramps rather than killers.[7] In writing about Robert Burns, one author describes the caves of the area:

Smuggling, generally of illicit brandy and other alcohol, was endemic in Scotland. In his native Ayrshire, there are legendary tales of cannibals who lived in coastal caves, which were merely a device intended to deter prying eyes while contraband was moved under cover of darkness—the exception being the real-life, flesh-tearing Sawney Bean and his notorious cannibal family from before (Robert) Burn's time.[8]

An 1864 description of the cave casts it in a less glamorous light, and makes no mention of the Beans at all: '[It is] impossible to form any opinion as to the purpose for which this rude place of strength has been intended'.[9]

There is evidence to suggest that, at one time, it was used as a prison by the Laird of Bennane,[10] while another local legend maintains that a piper lost his way in its penetrating depths and was heard piping beneath the hearthstone of the nearby Troax farmhouse.[11] Some claim that that the mournful wails of the bagpipes can still be heard.

To reach this cave from the road is treacherous at best, because it is under a steep incline, and a tall fence has recently been erected by local officials to prevent exploration, partly because deep holes in the floor of the cavern make any expedition by amateurs risky.

The entrance to the cave is almost impossible to see, a narrow crack in the jagged rock façade, blocked by a boulder. The interior has been sprayed with graffiti. The cave is alleged to extend nearly a mile into the rocky hill, but by all accounts those passages are hardly the vast rooms and lofty chambers described in *The Grey Man*, but tight, twisting cracks in the walls.

Why did Samuel Crockett Pick This Cave?

A close friend of Samuel Crockett, the well published local historian Reverend Roderick Lawson, wrote a book in 1892 on the Girvan area and provides the first real history of the cave. Revd Lawson was a minister in Maybole and an extensively published expert on Ayrshire and Galloway. He makes no mention of Sawney Bean whatsoever. Revd Lawson exchanged correspondence with Samuel Crockett,[12] and may have supplied the latter with information about the Bennane Head at Balcreuchan Port with a view to inspiring a fictional location for the novel only.

But the cave does not match the description either in Crockett's *The Grey Man* or in the chapbooks that preceded it. The high tide does make access to the cave from the shore nearly impossible, but it does not flood into it; and there are no large chambers where the Beans could have processed and dried human flesh for consumption. Locals who believe

The Cimmerian Den

One of the earliest images of the rocky outcropping where the Beans allegedly hid, in Revd Roderick Lawson's *Places of Interest About Girvan with Glimpses of Carrick History* (Paisley: J. and R. Parlane, 1892).

the story argue that the cave has collapsed over the centuries, burying the evidence of the Beans' nefarious activities.[13]

Alternatives

At least two alternative locations in Ayrshire and Galloway have been put forward in attempt to demarcate the Beans, neither more credible than the aforementioned.

One author places the cave in Rhins, but does not elaborate further.

> The coastline here is dotted with caves, so perhaps one should be claimed as the Rhins retreat of that commit-ted troglodyte, Sawney Bean, the shining star in the firmament of mythical Scottish rogues, whom at least one writer, John Wilson of Gatehouse, wanted to place in the southern Rhins.[14]

The other alternative, appearing in a local pamphlet in the Ewart Library in Dumfries, locates the Beans' cave on the Mull of Galloway.[15]

8
Adopting an English Story for Scottish Lore

Today, whenever Scotchmen gather together to celebrate their national identity, they assert it openly by certain distinctive national apparatus. They wear the kilt, woven in a tartan whose colour and pattern indicates their 'clan'; and if they indulge in music, their instrument is the bagpipe. This apparatus, to which they ascribe great antiquity, is in fact largely modern. It was developed after, sometimes long after, the Union with England against which it is, in a sense, a protest. Before the Union, it did indeed exist in vestigial form; but that form was regarded by the large majority of Scotchmen as a sign of barbarism: the badge of roguish, idle, predatory, blackmailing Highlanders who were more of a nuisance than a threat to civilised, historic Scotland. And even in the Highlands, even in that vestigial form, it was relatively new: it was not the original, or the distinguishing badge of Highland society. Indeed, the whole concept of a distinct Highland culture and tradition is a retrospective invention. Before the later years of the seventeenth century, the Highlanders of Scotland did not form a distinct people.[1]

Folklore Becomes Reality?

Folklore traditionally follows the following, designated path: it begins with a local story with some basis in reality; it then spreads to a broader audience, and integrates influences from outside of its region of origin; transformed, it finally re-enters its culture of origin, and becomes a part of its societal fabric.

Sawney Bean does not fit within this pattern in the least. The story was an alien invention, born outside of the region where it was set; it then became widely accepted as truth, without the least relation to the local culture of its setting; and finally, it was adopted by locals as their own. As a piece of folklore, the Bean saga breaks all of the rules.

Sawney Bean's acceptance by a substantial part of the population, if tongue-in-cheek, has much to do with business—tourists do travel to Galloway to see where the Beans lived. And in appropriating the story, some Galwegians have themselves edited the narrative, for instance in the Dumfries Variants kept in the Ewart Library in Dumfries. These are two hand-typed copies of the Bean saga, dated to between 1920 and 1950, and intended to provide local tourists with a summary of the affairs associated with the Beans.

Saunie Bane

Sauine Bane wis the sin o' a respectable ditcher and hedger in East Lothian: bit he couldna'e stan wark, and took up wi' a wumman o' no' very great character, and awa' aff wi' her tae a cave on the Mull o' Galloway, whaur they leeved be robbin', and eatin', the traivellers passin anywhere near. The kintra fowk wis sair troubled at sae many disappearances, and a when innkeepers alang the roads nearby wis hangit, fowk thinkin' the traivellers had been murthered by thame: but still traivellers disappeared: and hardly an inn wis open for miles aroon, which played intal the Banes' hauns,— an by noa Sawney and his wumman had a hale tribe o' weans, and the weans had grown up and had bairns o' their ain. Weel, a fairmer, and his wife ahint him on the pillion o' their powny, wur returnin ae day frae a fair, and evenin cam on, and a crood o' Banes burst up suddenly frae the muir room theame. The fairmer focht back wi' sword and pistol and rade some o' them doon: but they pu'd the puir wife frae the pillion: the Bane weeman cut her throat and drank her bluid, and than ripped her open and pu'd oot a' her entrails. The fairmer made ae brainge and gat clean awa', fur noo a pairty o' thirty or fowrty frae the same fair cam up and the Banes made awa'. The pairty saw the murthered wumman's corp and haird the fairmer's tale, and took whim wi' theme tae Glescae to tell't the Maginstrates, wha sent tae the King, James the First. He cam doon wi' three or fowre hunner men and searched the shore wi' bloodhoonds: they had missed the mooth o' the cave whum the dogs fun' in and raised sic a howlin' and yelpin that the King and his men, awa' on alang the strand, hard them and cam stoorin' bck.... Weel they lit torches and went haulf a mile intae the cave, and fun' the Banes and great stores o' dried and pickled legs, arms, thighs, hands and feet o' men, weemen and bairns hung up or steepin' in brine-tubs: and a mass of money, gowd and siller wi' watches, rings, swords, pistols and clothes. The Banes by noo nummered fifty-echt. Sawney and his wummen, echt sins, sax dochters, echteen graunsons and fowrteen graundochters. A' sur seized: the King and his men buried the remains o' their victims in the saun and took the Banes tae Edinburgh. They kept them the nicht in the Tolbooth and the next day executed thame a' wi' oot ony trial. The men hid their hauns and legs cut off and left tae bleed tae daith: the weeman and bairns, hivin;' watched this were burnt in three saiveral fires, a' cursin tae their laust gasp.[2]

While written in crude form, the author most likely had access to the Nicholson version of the Bean saga, since they refer only to King James I. Sawney is spelt in several different ways, which suggests that the author was influenced by another written copy at the time that they wrote this.

This version indicates that the Beans lived on the Mull of Galloway, the southernmost point of Scotland, at the end of a long narrow peninsula. Today it is home to a lighthouse and little else, and in the sixteenth century would have simply been a rocky outcropping. This detail is intriguing, because it only appears in the two Dumfries variants of the tale.

The second Dumfries account, writing by A. E. Truckell, is easier to read and offers new details that don't appear elsewhere.

Dumfries and Galloway Traditions—Sawnie Bane

Alexander Bane was the son of a respectable ditcher and hedger in the county of Haddingtonshire: but he fell into the company of a woman of ill repute and went off with her, settling in a remote part of the Galloway shore (some say the Mull, some the Carrick shore of Fleet Bay.)

There they occupied a cave and lived by robbing and eating passers-by. They had a large family, and as these grew up brother married sister and begat still more Banes.

The effect of this cannibalistic colony had long been felt in the surrounding country: so many wayfarers had disappeared that suspicion fell on innkeepers in the area, and several were hung: but still the disappearances continued.

Finally, one evening as dusk was falling, a farmer was returning on his pony from Laureneekirk Fair, his wife on the pillion behind him, when suddenly a crowd of Banes rose up out of the moorland around them. The farmer defended himself desperately but despite his efforts his wife was torn from the pillion. In an instant her throat was cut, the Banes, men and women, were drinking her blood with as great a gust as it had been whine: (according to Nicolson who tells the tale with mid-Victorian gusto), and she was ripped open and her entrails torn out. At this the farmer made a final desperate lunge and broke away, just as a large party of country folk also returning from the Fair came up. The Banes scattered, leaving the woman's corpse. On hearing the farmer's account the whole party made for Glasgow, where they notified the magistrates, who sent to King James the First. King James with a large body of armed men came down and searched the coast, but to no avail. They had passed an apparently shallow cave-mouth and were far down the shore, thinking of abandoning their search, when they heard the bloodhounds they had brought with them baying and whining at the mouth of the cave. They entered and found that after a narrow and tortuous entrance it widened. After penetrating for a mile and a half they entered a great chamber, and there they found the Banes—plus many human limbs in steep-tubs, or hanging smoked on hooks—and tubs and boxes full of watches, rings, pistols, snuff boxes and jewellery. The Banes were secured, the limbs decently buried in the sand at the mouth of the cave, and the party returned to Edinburgh. There it was felt that the Banes hardly deserved a trial: so all the Bane men were burned in a great fire, while the women and children watched. These then had their hands and feet cut off and bled to death. So ended the Banes.'

And what of the tale? The bones of it are clearly very old: a little inbred clan living in isolation, preying on travellers and practicing cannibalism in the Bronze Age or Iron Age: James I of Scotland and the punishment (clearly for heresy—cannibalism was heresy) are medaeval additions: the watches, snuff-boxes and the ditcher-and-hedger father are more recent still. The whole is a good example of how a traditional tale is brought up to date.[3]

This version of the Bean story is interesting on several fronts. It no longer alludes to East Lothian in general, but narrows Sawney Bean's place of origin down to Haddingtonshire. While this doesn't entirely help with identifying the Beans further, this addition implies research on the author's part.

The reference to the Laureneekirk Fair is interesting too, since this was a well-established fair actually located in Laurencekirk, which is on the northeast coast of Scotland—impossible to reconcile with the rest of the Bean story. If the farmer and his wife were ambushed coming from Laurencekirk, the Beans would have had to flee across the entire width of Scotland to reach their cave in Galloway. The fair would have brought the farmer closer to Edinburgh, too, so why not simply go there instead of Glasgow?

The demise of the Beans is also altered here: the men are burned, and the women and children bled to death. This is either a misinterpretation of the Nicholson version of the story—a simple swapping of roles—or the result of the story's gradual mutation over time.

Girvan and the Hairy Tree

Perhaps the most precise localisation of the Bean story was attempted in the late twentieth and early twenty-first century with the legend of the Hairy Tree, when a local journalist in Ayrshire began to promote an addition to the tale. According to this new myth, the tree was planted by Sawney Bean's eldest daughter in the town of Girvan, on Dalrymple Street. Depending on what version of the story you read, she either took up residence in Girvan, having abandoned her family's murderous ways, or was apprehended with them in the cave by King James VI and I.

Upon the Beans' arrest, she was not taken to the Tolbooth in Edinburgh with the others, but back to Girvan, where she was supposedly hanged from the very tree that she had planted. In this new twist, people for years after her death heard the sound of a corpse swinging in the wind if they stood under this tree. The tree allegedly disappeared, and its exact location has been lost over time. Another local journalist, Andrew Penguin, has run a campaign to try and locate where the Hairy Tree had grown.

Girvan is a quaint seaside town just north of Bennane Head. The town was not founded until the seventeenth century, and was at that time inhabited by either farmers or fishermen.[4] Nowhere in its historical texts are there references to the Bean family, or the Hairy Tree. In fact, outside of the internet and some local coverage, no reference to the Hairy Tree can be found prior to 1998.

If such a tree had existed, it would have been at the southern end of Girvan, near the Toll—the jail of the town, which was only built in the eighteenth century.

There is one obvious flaw in the story of the Hairy Tree: the Bean woman hanging from the very tree she planted may have poetic irony, but it does not stand up to the known facts. Hangings and executions in Girvan took place at its Moot Hill, or as it was known, the 'Hill of Judgment'—'Here tales of blood were recounted, plans of revenge concerted: here foes were put to their death'.[5] It seems odd that one of Sawney's daughters would be executed anywhere else.

Then again, the tale of the Hairy Tree has as little tangible evidence to credit it as the rest of the Sawney Bean folklore.

There are two possible explanations for the accrual of this subplot; one is that the idea of the Hairy Tree was locally conceived, and as such became easily adjoined to the Bean tale; the other is that the Girvan community realised the business value of such an association.

The Deen Pamphlet

Sawney Bean was again given a firm location in a pamphlet published by Glasgow author Ron Deen. This booklet, *On The Trail of Sawney Bean and his Cannibal Family*, is twelve pages long, and recounts Deen's forty-five-year exploration of the validity of—and ultimate rejection of— the Bean tale.[6] His search still leads him to the same Bennane Head cave, and its limited exploration. Deen claims he found bones in the cave, which he is supposed to have buried in the sands rather than turn over to the authorities. The booklet is useful in that it provides directions to the cave site, apparently to assist potential tourists.

Deen's pamphlet adds credibility to the Bean legend by highlighting one of the few tangible elements of the myth—a physically real cave. Doing so only seems to have fuelled Bean tourism further. As scholars Sandy Hobbs and David Cornwell contend,

> When tourism appears to affect the popularity or character of local lore, as may be the case with the Sawney Bean story, we are not dealing with a corruption or a distortion of a 'real' story, but rather with a coming together of different cultures. Tourists are folk. The interaction of tourist and local lore is no less worthy of serious consideration than other comings together of two cultures.[7]

9

Was There a Real Alexander Bean?

Sawney Beane and his family, by John Nicholson, is a gorgeous piece of black macabre, told in that wonderful style of understatement which some Victorians writers handled so well. You may completely dismiss any shred of comfort from your mind that it is some far-fetched yarn concocted by a mad writer in the final stages of delirium tremors, for it is, in every detail, perfectly true.[1]

For cannibalistic murders to have occurred, there must have been a murderer: one Alexander Bean. 'Bean' has plethora of different spellings: 'Bane', 'Bean' (the traditional Scottish spelling), 'Bain', 'Beane' (the English variant of the name), 'Been', 'MacBean', and 'Bein' are all accepted variants of the name.

Searching for Alexander Bean—or indeed any Beans—who might have lived between 1567 and 1603 is complicated by several factors: documentation is scarce, because literacy was then still limited, usually to members of the church; and formal census records were generations away from coming into wide usage, and besides fail to tell the complete story of the men and women recorded.

The most accessible source of family history are old parish and Catholic Church registers from the seventeenth century. These materials, preserved by the National Register of Records of Scotland, cover the births, deaths, marriages, and wills of the period. Fortunately, there were actually very few Beans on record in the period of in question (with all of their variation spellings). The following details what I have been able to discover in these records.

Alexander Bean, Beane, and Bane

There were several Alexander Beans living after the period in question, who have been related to a potential Sawney. While we do not have the birth record for the first, we do know that he was married to Helene Hutown, lived in Dunfermline (not far from Edinburgh), and had several children, including a son named Alexander. Alexander and Helene's children were born as follows:

Jonet Bean	23 April 1613
Williame Bean	2 February 1617
Alexander Bean	22 August 1619
Issobel Bean	22 January 1622[2]

Alexander is also recorded to have had another child, Johne, born on 30 December 1610, with Margaret Hutown.[3]

The parish records indicate that a Sandy Beane was born on 30 January 1616, but the father was not listed;[4] 'Sandy' is a variant of 'Sawney', so this birth record is potentially important as well. Sandy Beane was also born in Dunfermline, the same town and parish that Alexander and Helene lived in, so it can be assumed with relative safety that they were somehow related.

Likewise, an Alexander Beane, son of Allaster Beane and Christine Freman, was also born in Dunfermline, on 29 November 1618.[5]

An Issobel Beane married William Chalmers on 18 June 1618 in Edinburgh, but there is no clear connection between this Issobel and the Dunfermline Issobel born in 1622, nor are there records of Issobel having any children.

Two Alexander Banes lived in the same period, but neither came from East Lothian—both their families were based in Inverness. One was born on 2 May 1619, the son of Johne Beane and Issobel Wilkie, and the other on 22 June 1595, son of Raynold Bane and Jonet Douglas.[6]

We must dismiss the possibility, tantalizing as it is, that any of these men might have been Sawney Bean. They were far too young to have spent twenty-five years in Galloway and be apprehended by James VI and I, and even if we were to stretch the window of time until the end of King James's rule (1625), other factors raise issues. For instance, the only record of these candidates was found in church records, and one must wonder whether the Bean family would indeed have been members in good standing? In light of the religious upheaval of the period, and the communal culture of surveillance and paranoia arisen from witch-hunting, avoiding church would have been a rarity. According to the folklore, Sawney's parents were respected, hard-working, so probably would have been church-goers who would have had the birth recorded.

There are, of course, records missing from the period as well. If Sawney was not one of these Beans, Beanes, or Banes, then perhaps his records were simply lost, if they ever existed in the first place.

All that this line of research does establish is that an Alexander Bean did live somewhere in Scotland at the time most likely to correspond with the legend, and that the name was not uncommon. One might speculate as to how members of the Bean family reacted when the story went into print, not least those with an Alexander in their family tree!

Part Three

SAWNEY BEAN'S LEGACY

Peter Locke's and Wes Craven's horror film, *The Hills Have Eyes*, based on the character of Sawney Bean. (*Peter Locke*)

10

The Folklore Grows

> The traveller on his weary way
> By us beset implores in vain.
> His eye-lid soon shut out the day
> His pallid cheek ne'er blooms again
> Beguiling gold thy gilded power
> Bids from the bosom duty fly;
> Arrests ambitions fleeting hour
> And boldly bids the robber die.[1]

The folklore became more widely accepted in the nineteenth century. Plays on the Beans' terrorisation of southern Scotland came into production: *Sawney Bean, the Terror of the North*, performed at the Royal Coburg Theatre on 18 February 1823; *Sawney Beane* or *Harlequin and the Man Eater*, a pantomime performed at Sadler's Wells Theatre, Islington, on 1 April 1839; and *Sawney Bean, the Cannibal*, performed at the City of London Theatre on 20 April 1864.[2]

In 1970, Robert Nye and Bill Watson's play, *Sawney Bean*, explored the metaphysical dimensions of Sawney.

> Like all great myths, this beautiful and powerful fable, based on the true story of the eighteenth-century Galloway cannibal, touches the reader's primal instincts and responds to his deepest needs for artistic expression. The characters are essentially timeless: the semi-articulate Sawney, who creates a poignant image of innocence before the fall: his loyal wife, Lila, whom he finally sacrifices; Jot and Rain, who represent different elements of nature; and Solomon, Sawney's spiritual son, who eventually develops a will of his own.[3]

Beyond the title, this bears little resemblance to the legend. Sawney is portrayed as a violent but misunderstood figure, and for anyone familiar with the folklore, it is difficult to conceive of him in a sympathetic role.

In Novel Form

Samuel Crockett wasn't the first or last novelist to transport Sawney Bean into literature, though he was the most successful. In 1844, the novel *Sawney Bean: The Man-Eater of Midlothian* was published, the copy of which at the British Library was unfortunately destroyed several years ago. This version pre-dates Crockett's *The Grey Man*, but its relatively short print run testifies to its comparatively meagre popularity.

L. A. Morse's *The Flesh Eaters*, published in 1979, sports a Frank Frazetta cover and focuses on the horror of the tale, which begins in 1408; in the opening of the book, the author contends

> Though 'The Flesh Eaters' does contain speculative elements, the essentials are historical fact. Sawney Beane was a real person who lived in Scotland during the first half of the fifteenth century. In a cave not far from Edinburgh, he and his woman raised their huge and terrifying family. Their way of life, their means of existence, and the manner of their deaths are truly depicted here.[4]

Morse goes on to quote John Nicolson, one suspects for the sake of credibility.

Novelist Harry Tait approached the Beans very differently in his novel, *The Ballad of Sawney Bain*. He begins with Sawney's confession to a priest, which lays the foundation for how the Beans fell into their lives of crime. Sawney remains unrepentant of consuming human flesh, which he was forced to do.[5] In Frieda Gates's book, *Sawney Beane: The Abduction of Elspeth Cumming*, Sawney's story is told from the perspective of a young woman whom the Beans take prisoner.[6]

Novelists have the tendency to launch their narratives with a declaration of the story's historical authenticity, and that they are merely expanding on it. But they are not alone in this: many historians have done the same, lifting 'facts' from previous prints of the Bean folklore and converting them into truisms, for instance in the *Scottish Tales of Terror*,[7] or the *Great Short Stories of Detection, Mystery and Horror*.[8]

The World's Strangest Crimes is little more helpful in its confusingly dualistic assessment.

> From time to time in the course of human history natural depravity plumbs new depths—and not only during wars. The Sawney Beane case in the early seventeenth century concerned a family that lived in a cave and chose murder, cannibalism and incest as its way of life. For twenty-five years this family, rejecting all accepted standards of human behaviour

and morality, carried on a vicious guerrilla war against humanity. Even a medieval world accustomed to torture and violence was horrified ... the story itself is simple enough, though scarcely credible, and has been well authenticated....[9]

Contemporary true crime novels chronicle the story of the Beans as true. Colin Wilson and Patricia Pitman's *Encyclopaedia of Murder* in 1961 treat the story as true, citing Nicholson as the source. Wilson and Pitman place the tale somewhere between the years 1360 and 1430, and alter the number of people coming back from the fair from a large group to six.[10]

In the Twentieth Century

The Bean tale has become more graphic and visually violent with the advent of new media, and has since been distributed to a much broader audience. Gone is the age when text alone must convey the horrors of the story.

One example of a popular twentieth-century adaptation is the comic book genre, which has allowed younger readers who might never have heard of to the Bean story to form their own opinions. In 1976, the Beans appeared in a D.O.A Comics issue set between 1390 and 1437. While this was only an underground comic, it did perpetuate the legend outside of Scotland.

The first homage on film to the legend of Sawney and his family was the 1974 vintage horror film, *The Texas Chainsaw Massacre*. The film follows a band of friends who fall prey to a family of cannibals while on their way to visit an old homestead. The killers are led by the aptly named Leatherface. The Texas Chainsaw Massacre ushered in a new age of horror films—the 'slasher' genre—the main canvass of which was young teenage victims being gruesomely slaughtered—hillbilly cannibal killers in particular became a trend in the 1970s. The film was marketed as a 'true story' inspired not by Sawney and his clan, but by the real-life serial killer Ed Gein. While the director and producer have never claimed a connection to Sawney, insinuations of cannibalism persist: Leatherface hangs his victims on meat hooks, has furniture made of human bones, and part of the setting is an old abandoned slaughterhouse. Conversely, Ed Gein's only true link to the film was that he wore a mask made out of a human scalp and face—as opposed to Leatherface's leather mask—was known to wear a body suit made of female body parts, and used his victim's body parts and skin to decorate his home—including for seat covers and a belt made of female nipples. Gein robbed graveyards for some of these parts, while others were taken from his victims. Gein swore that he did not eat his victims, but the fact that the authorities made such an enquiry says something about the nature of his crimes. In any case, one would be strained to determine exactly how much either Bean or Gein influenced the film.

The 1970s proved a major decade for more overt adaptations of the Bean story to the big screen. Sawney Bean's biggest leap and endorsement was the 1977 'B'-class horror film *The Hills Have Eyes*, which centres on a travelling family stranded in the Californian desert becoming the prey of feral cannibals living in a filthy cave. This is in many respects a perfect mirror of the Bean story, as director Wes Craven and producer Peter Locke reveal was their intention:

> Craven: 'I resisted [doing another horror film] until I was broke. And finally Peter [Locke] said my wife's out in Vegas and we can do something out in the desert. And just come out and write something for the desert. So I went to the New York Public Library and went to their Murder and Mayhem division and ran across the story of the Sawney Bean family. Which I think was a sixteenth or seventeenth century family that was cannibalistic, that would prey on travellers.'
> Locke: 'They were like highwaymen but worse.'
> Craven: 'They would eat the horses, they would eat the people and everything. And they lived in a cave that was on a cliff facing the sea.'
> Locke: 'At high tide you couldn't find them because the water came in and there was no trace of where they lived.'
> Craven: 'Finally they were found by a survivor that ran away and went to the King and the King sent an expedition. The expedition found them and took them back to London and they did horrendous things to them. They broke them all on the wheel, they hanged the women in front of the men, and they dismembered the men. And I was so struck by how on one hand you have this feral family that's killing people and eating them, but if you look at it, they weren't doing anything that much worse than what civilisation did to them when they caught them. And I just thought wow, what a great kind of A B of culture. How the most civilized can be the savage; and how the most savage can be the most civilized.'
> Locke: 'That was the basis of The Hills Have Eyes.'[11]

The success of this film and its ensuing franchise created a demand for the core elements of the Bean story in horror audiences everywhere. More and more films have borrowed from the themes of the Bean story: in 1973, *The Wicker Man*; in 2003, *Evil Breed: The Legend of Samhain*; and in 2006, *Hillside Cannibals*. In 2006, Wes Craven returned to the premise

The Folklore Grows 133

US rock band 'Sawney Bean' in the 1970s. (*Author's collection*)

The legend is brought back to the screen in *Sawney Bean, Flesh of Man*. (*Philaberg Films*)

SAWNEY BEANS RESTAURANT

SAWNEY BEAN was believed to have been the last known cannibal in Britain and is understood to have lived with his family in a cave in South West Scotland.

The disappearance of travellers who were ambushed by the Sawney Bean clan in the area led to the whole family being rounded up by King James VI who required 400 men to do the job. The gruesome family were taken to Edinburgh where they were executed.

The pictures around our restaurant highlight the story of Sawney Bean.

Welcome to Sawney Beans. We hope you will enjoy your visit to our restaurant. We have tried to offer traditional fayre using fresh local produce where possible.

The menu from Sawney Bean's Restaurant in Dumfries.

and produced a prequel, *The Hills Have Eyes: The Beginning*. The 2008 Scottish horror film *Sacrificed* was also based on the Beans. In 2013, *Sawney: Flesh of Man* was released in the UK. One thing is certain: the folklore of the cannibals in the cave has been profitable.

Beyond the screen, other forms of media have inadvertently spread the story. In the 1970s, a short-lived American rock band took the name Sawney Bean; the punk rock band The Real McKenzies performed a song called 'Sawney Beane Clan' in their 1995 debut album; Snakefinger's 1987 album *Night of Desirable Objects* featured the 'Ballad of Sawney Bean.' By the late twentieth century, the Beans were more widely—if not directly—known than at any point in their long and sordid history.

The Beans have been embraced by the people they allegedly tormented generations earlier—Galwegians have embraced the legend as reality. Today in Dumfries the bar/restaurant named 'Sawney Bean's' boasts water-coloured paintings from the story of the Bean tale at each of its tables. In Steinbach, Canada, former residents of Stranraer have opened up 'Sawney Bean's Pub'. Both restaurants' names are strange choices—plausibly akin to naming an establishment after Ted Bundy, Charles Manson, or the Yorkshire Ripper, some may argue. Who knows, perhaps with the passage of time, these firmly real infamous killers will they too be commemorated in the same manner?

The tourist trade and the Bean folklore are ever more hopelessly intertwined, as a result of which, reality and the legend continue to be confused. For years, the London Dungeon Wax Museum has maintained a wax figure of Sawney Bean, lending further weight to the concept of him as a historical—rather than fictional—figure. The 1973 edition of the Guinness Book of World Records lists Sawney Bean as one of history's most prolific killers. Finally, the Edinburgh Dungeon hosts highly elaborate Sawney Bean performances, at the end of which visitors are invited to assist the King's men in the clan's capture! Guests board a boat which takes them on an atmospheric journey to the 'Bean Cave': they are greeted by the Bean children and led into their lair, where performers accost them with 'I want to pickle you!' At the last moment, the King arrives and arrests Sawney Bean, and the cannibals tell the guests to flee so that they can save themselves.[12]

The Sceptics

Despite the authors at Guinness, the truth of the tale has been questioned for centuries. As early as 1829, one writer's research leads them to express doubt in a letter to the editor of *Gentleman's Magazine*.

The atrocities at Edinburgh by the wretches Burke and Hare, aided by two females, will naturally recall to the minds of some of your readers, the atrocities said to have been perpetrated in former ages in that part of the kingdom; which, however incredible they may formally have appeared, are not more so than the crimes which have been lately proved and confessed.

One of the most remarkable is the history of Sawny Bean and his family. This wholesales trading murderer is said to have been a native of Tranent in East Lothian, and to have been guilty of an offense which obliged him to leave that part of the country; when he betook himself and family to a cave on the coast of Galloway, opposite to Ireland; and they derived their subsistence from robbery and murder, chiefly during the night. They are said to have carried the bodies to their cave, and to have eaten then up. This abominable work is said to have gone on for many years; and the family is said to have multiplied during the time, and all of them to have adopted this mode of subsistence. At last, attacking a person who effected his escape, a military forces was sent out against them by King James VI. When they were tracked out by bloodhounds, taken, tried, and executed. In the cave limbs of human bodies are said to have been found hanging up, cured and dried.

This narrative is found in many popular works; and in that part of the country where the events are said to have taken place, is believed as an article of faith. On the latter circumstance I do not place much reliance, having discovered, both in this and foreign countries, instances where well-told fictitious narrative has created an impression, which, in a short while after, has produced an apparent corroborative tradition. Still it is possible, and perhaps probable, that there were some remarkable atrocities which produced popular horror, and consequent terrific exaggeration.

Will any of your Correspondents inform you of the earliest work, in which the above narrative, or any to which it refers, appears; and whether there be any authentic record whatever, of anything which took place before the Courts. It would be curious and instructive to view the original real figure, which has been magnified into so horrific a monster by the magic-lantern of popular imagination, and love of the wonderful and terrible.[13]

This letter sets the premise that by 1829, the Sawney Bean tale was already accepted by the people of Galloway as truth—long before the publication of *The Grey Man*. It equally makes the point that research into the matter had been conducted for centuries, and thus far yielded nothing.

In 1934, William Roughead wrote a historical book of crime, *Rogues*

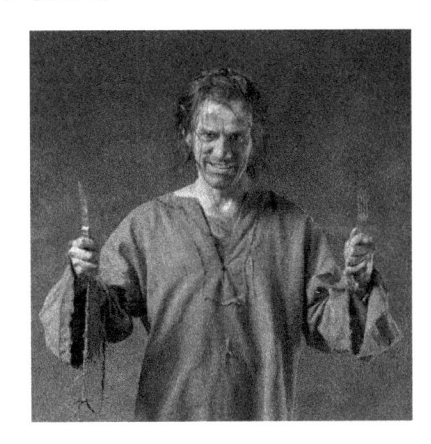

Sawney Bean reenacted on a living stage at the Edinburgh Dungeon. (*The Edinburgh Dungeon, Merlin Entertainments Group*)

Walk Here, in which he methodically dissects John Nicholson's account, pointing out the flaws and evidential gaps. He comes to the following, prosaic conclusion:

> And now, discarding the historian's gown and divesting myself of the partial garb of the biographer, as a mere irresponsible mortal I have something for the reader's private ear. We have heard, on what is claimed to be unimpeachable authority, an account of the sanguinary life and death of Sawney Beane. We have before us what purports to be an authentic portrait of the man, complete with the cave and the victim, his prudent spouse carrying in a brace of joints, his industrious issue drive him fresh supplies for the family larder. But, after all, with respect to my hero's personality, I must confess myself of counsel with Mrs. Prig in her immortal dictum touching the identity of Mrs. Harris: 'I don't believe there's no such person!' Notwithstanding that Captain Johnson in his goodly folio sets forth the 'facts' with a vraisemblance and wealth of circumstance worthy of Defoe—who maintained that 'lies are not worth a farthing if they are not calculated for the effectual deceiving of the people they are designed to deceive.'—I am driven to the conclusion that all these things, like the verbal embroideries of Pooh-Bah, must be regarded as 'merely corroborative detail, intended to give artistic verisimilitude to a bald and unconvincing narrative.' And the cause of my scepticism is this: I have sought diligently for Sawney in the official records of the time, in contemporary journals, diaries, and memoirs, in the pages of gossiping annalists and of grave historians; and I have failed to find either in print or manuscript the slightest mention of him.[14]

Finally, in 1975 Ronald Holmes wrote *The Legend of Sawney Bean*, which sought to prove or disprove the tale once and for all. The book has

Watercolour image of the Bean family attacking the farmer and his wife in Sawney Bean's Restaurant in Dumfries—the perfect image for a relaxing meal!

become a cult-classic for Bean enthusiasts, and while it is a difficult read, Holmes goes far to demonstrate the remarkable dearth of evidence. He maintains that English authors penned the story as a deliberate slur of the Scots, but concedes that this has not prevented it from embedding itself in Galwegian culture.

> The legend portrays Sawney Bean as a criminal and mass-murderer who was executed about the year 1600. There are, however, no records or other supporting evidence to prove that he really existed. This book is a work of detection which sets out to solve a murder mystery but, in so doing, displays Sawney Bean not so much as a criminal but as a primeval presence from the dark past of the human mind.[15]

Yet winning the argument is not possible when dealing with folklore: the Bean saga will forever elude a decisive categorisation in either the factual or fictional camp, simply because it cannot easily be disproven.

Another watercolour of Sawney Bean's restaurant in Dumfries—King James VI leads the bloodhounds in search of the Beans.

As contemporary historians Sandy Hobbs and David Cornwell have more recently put it,

> We suggest that, like all successful legends, it must be a 'good' story, otherwise it would not survive. The telling must be rewarding to both the teller and the audience. We have already discussed how the story could come to be acceptable to Scots. That acceptability will be enhanced if it gets a good reaction when told. What aspect of this story is likely to produce a favourable reaction from tourists? Cannibalism is dramatic. Historical distance avoids any implication of present danger. There is also the general feature of tourist lore that a good story about a particular location helps to justify the traveller's decision to visit it.[16]

11

The Devil's in the Details

Scot mothers were telling recalcitrant children if they were not good and did not do as they were told, Sawney Bean would get them.[1]

There are a few remaining strands of Sawney Bean that must be addressed one by one. The best source for doing this is the most accepted version of the tale, John Nicholson's (Appendix E).

'His father was a hedger and ditcher and brought up his sons to the same laborious employment.' Yet while these occupations were common in Nicholson's own lifetime, most historians agree that they were not likely to have existed at the time at which Bean could have existed: '… it is unlikely that anyone specialised at those occupation in Scotland of the 15th and 16th Centuries'.[2]

'… he left his father and mother, and ran way into the desert part of the country, taking with him a woman as viciously inclined as himself.' The internet has recently identified Sawney's wife as 'Black Agnes', a name coincidentally shared by a real person, Agnes Randolph, Countess of Dunbar and March—best known for her defence of Dunbar Castle against an English attack in 1338. The real Black Agnes was a heroine of Scottish history, whose association with the Bean story is non-existent, merely the product of poor research and speculation. She lived in the wrong time period, and had no links whatsoever to the Bean tale.

'They never kept any company but among themselves, and supported themselves wholly by robbing: being, moreover so very cruel, that they never robbed any one, whom they did not murder.' This part of the narrative deserves more scrutiny because it contains a contradiction. If the Beans subsisted on their robberies, they surely would have had to go into town to sell their loot, or if they didn't, one wonders why they bothered to rob their victims at all? Although this may plausibly be explained by their cannibalism, in that that would have been their first priority, this passage still—its wording unchanged in most accounts—emphasises robbery as their *raison d'être*.

'The number of people these savages destroyed was never exactly known; but it was generally computed that in the twenty-five years they continued their butcheries, they had washed their hands with the blood of at least a thousand men, women and children.' The demographic figures for Galloway are difficult to calculate, but its population has been estimated at 40,000 by AD 1000.[3] The population of Ayrshire, where the Beans' alleged cave was in most accounts located, was estimated at 50,000 in the sixteenth century.[4] This renders the common claim that, 'the whole country was almost depopulated' highly dubious. Clearly, it could not have been.

'… his majesty in person, with a body of about four hundred men, set out for the place where this dismal tragedy was acted, in order to search all of the rocks and thickets, that, if possible, they might apprehend this hellish crew, which had so long pernicious been to all western parts of the kingdom.' King James VI and I was one of the most documented regents of his era, yet no evidence exists of this threat. According to Scottish historian Dr Louise Yeoman, King James was a very keen hunter, but was unlikely to have put himself in danger by leading this perilous trek; in any case, he would have been sure to widely publish the news of life-threatening situations, like he did the Gunpowder Plot. 'If James had successfully led an expedition to face down a well-armed group of bloodthirsty cannibals,' says Dr Yeoman, 'we would have never heard the end of it.'[5]

'…they took him [the assaulted man] with them to Glasgow, and told the affair to the magistrates of that city, who immediately sent to the king concerning it.' Glasgow would not have been the first place that the prisoners would have been taken—the closest royal burgh in Ayrshire was in Ayr and Irvine—and the Sheriff of Ayr, not the magistrates, would not have been consulted.[6] And, given the limitations of the sixteenth–century road network, the Beans would have had to go through Ayr on their way to Glasgow anyway, had they been apprehended on the shore.

'When they came to their journey's end, the wretches were committed to the Tolbooth […]'. Why march the Beans to the Tolbooth in Edinburgh when there were jail facilities in both Ayr[7] and Glasgow that could have held them prisoner? In any case, records of the Tolbooth in Edinburgh do not begin until 1657, so there are no means of verifying any potential Beans' captivity there.

'[…] the next day [they were] conducted, under a strong guard, to Leith, where they were executed without any process […]'. Why the march to Leith when the executions could have been conveniently taken care of just outside of the Tolbooth, where there was an execution platform handy?

'The men were dismembered, their hands and legs severed from their bodies by which amputation they bled to death in a few hours. The wife, daughters, and grand-children, having been made spectators of this just punishment inflicted on the man, were afterwards burnt to death in three several fires.' Such barbarous executions were only rarely carried out in Scotland in extreme cases, and even though the Bean case would have qualified, the costs for such a procedure would have left a trail in the burgh minute books or their account ledgers, yet no such record has come to light.

12
On Sawney Bean's Trail

The monstrous figure of Sawney, as written history, was probably an English invention. Cannibalism has a long history as a means of political propaganda used by a dominant culture against those they want to colonise; as an English invention, Sawney may be considered a colonial fiction written to demonstrate the savagery and uncivilised nature of the Scots in contrast to the superior qualities of the English nation.[1]

It is a natural curiosity that draws someone to see the sites and visit the locations associated with historic events—even the mass-murdering cannibalism of the Bean family. Many locals don't want tourism in the Ayrshire and Galloway region to thrive on retracing Sawney's footsteps.

What is most reprehensible about all this is that the myth is popularised as part of a despicable conspiracy of the heritage industry, tourist agencies and local authorities to turn parts of Scotland into little more than gruesome theme parks. If peddling the Sawney Bean story attracts tourists to Carrick, surely they are the wrong kind of tourists.[2]

Yet many people feel a need to associate the lore with a physical location.
The following is a list of the implicated locales which can be visited today, with respect for landowners and the local authorities, as well as few tips from myself.

Edinburgh, Ayr, Girvan, Bennane Head, and Dumfries

Perhaps the easiest place to begin is the Tolbooth in Edinburgh. It was here that they were held, legend has it, just prior to their execution at Leith. This was the central municipal building in Edinburgh for more than four centuries, built in 1403; the Old Tolbooth was used continuously until it

This circle on the Royal Mile in Edinburgh marks the location of the Tolbooth, where Sawney and his family were allegedly held prior to their execution.

was demolished in 1817. Locating the site of the Tolbooth is relatively easy. It is on Edinburgh's infamous Royal Mile, on the western end of the Luckenbooths on the High Street, and its site is marked by cobblestones. Five blocks away is the Edinburgh Dungeon, 31 Market Street, near the train station. Leith was the Edinburgh port where the Beans were supposedly executed and burned. It is has since been built up, but visitors can still walk along 'the Shore' or visit the 'Giant's Brae' on the Leith Links—an artillery battery in the lifetime of Mary Queen of Scots. If you want to see the original chapbooks associated with the Beans, these can be viewed at the National Library of Scotland at George IV Bridge. There are very stringent rules regarding the handling of these manuscripts, but it is a fascinating side-step worth making. Finally, there are the East Lothians, a region made up of distinct communities, none of which can specifically be tied to the Beans.

On the western coast of Scotland is Ayr, an excellent launching point for any expedition in search of the Beans' cave or the hairy tree. The Malt Cross restaurant and pub at 4-18 New Bridge Street now stands where witches were once burned to death. The remnants of the original Malt Cross can be inspected in the corner of the Carnegie Library, a short distance from the pub.

The tiny village of Girvan can be reached via the A 77 south of Ayr. The road brings you in parallel to Dalrymple Street, at the southern end of

Above and below: The earliest photographs of the main street of Girvan, where one of Sawney's daughters is supposed to have been hung from the Hairy Tree. (*South Ayrshire Libraries*)

which the hairy tree was supposedly planted and Sawney Bean's daughter hanged. Girvan is small and parking can be a bit tricky, but a visit offers a clearer picture of the scene of the hanging.

Access to the cave at Bennane Head is not practical during high tide, and extreme caution is advisable. The local authorities have made access to the cave difficult for a reason—namely, individuals have been injured attempting to reach the cave. You should only attempt this effort if you are physically able, preferably with another person. Heading south on the A 77, you will pass Bennane Head and come across a parking area along the coast. Chain link fencing has been put up to prevent would-be explorers from going down the steep walk to the shore, but it is still possible to do so. Once on the shore, turn back towards Bennane Head and you will see a narrow crack in the rock, obstructed by a four-foot tall boulder, so entrance is not easy. You will have to climb up on uneven ground to reach the cave. The cave also has rocky crevasses in the floor in the some spaces, so you will need a flashlight to even consider entering.

Dumfries itself does not directly figure in the legend, but it is one of the few communities that has openly embraced Sawney Bean as part of their folklore. There are two places where Sawney is commemorated in the town: the first is in the shopping district, in a WHSmith bookstore, 129-133 on the High Street—behind the sales counter is a mural of Galloway history and myth, which features an image of Sawney Bean. The second commemoration is Sawney Bean's Pub and Bistro at the corner of Hoods Loaning English Street and Bard's Corner; each booth in the hotel restaurant is adorned with a watercolour from the story; the food is traditional Scottish fare—no human parts included.

The End of the Trail

To come across that one perception-altering piece of evidence is the secret wish of every historian and true crime writer. My own multi-year journey into the saga of one of history's first alleged mass-murderers gave me tantalizing tit-bits, but nothing to put the proverbial meat on the bones (pun intended).

The Sawney Bean story will be with us for centuries. Incest, serial killers, cannibalism, the hint of the supernatural, and the horrific final justice … the truth does not matter, because these components appeal to the darker side of human nature, and in a multitude of forms.

No matter what evidence comes to light to disprove the legend, there will always be those who believe it to be true. In the 1980s, a local blacksmith and self-proclaimed psychic detective, Tom Robinson, claimed to have seen ghosts wandering the infamous cave where the Beans lived. He contended that the Beans never were taken to the Tolbooth in Edinburgh, but that they were sealed alive in there, condemned to a slow and agonizing death. He also claimed to have heard a woman's scream, and to have seen a female form dragged into the cave's recesses by twelve white lights, while a male figure lay immobile on the cave floor. Mr Robinson returned in 1991 to perform an exorcism on the cave, to give the ghostly victims some measure of peace.[3]

Ultimately, this is the tale of how folklore comes to maturity. In an ever increasingly connected world, anything can be posted to the internet, information can be changed, copied, and eventually accepted as fact with growing ease. A piece of folklore can accrue enough of a research trail on paper and online for it to indefinitely assume a factual guise, even for those closest to the story. This new paradigm for folklore evolution has no better example than Sawney Bean.

The Bean story has evolved from word of mouth, to chapbooks, to regional anthropology, to literature, the stage, and film, and to local business opportunity. It is impossible for us to determine beyond a doubt whether Sawney Bean's original authors had anti-Scottish propaganda in mind; but popularisation, and regional and national appropriation of the tale have rendered such qualms obsolete. The legend has transcended its political provenance.

Films like the *Silence of the Lambs* are the fruit of centuries of interest in the cannibal sociopath—is Hannibal Lecter really so different from Sawney Bean? Ironically, it now seems that Sawney Bean has actually become a precept that instils in such characters the semblance of credibility.

Other strands of Galwegian folklore—which boasts giants, ghosts, and witches—are also meant to have a footing in reality. For example, Janet Dalrymple, whose ghost is said to haunt Baldoon Castle, is supposed to have stabbed David Dunbar in her bridal chamber at Carsecleugh Castle because she wanted to marry Lord Rutherford, and to have ultimately gone insane. In actual fact, Janet and the Carsecleugh Castle did not really exist, but Dunbar was indeed murdered.

The Bean folklore is anchored by real locations, and the interventions of real historical figures, and so the story lives on. But in the end, does it matter if Sawney and his family ever truly existed? The evidence is paper-thin, but few of us would go for a night-time stroll in search of the cave at Bennane Head, let alone enter it. Why? Because while we know with every fibre of our being that Sawney is a myth, few of us would be willing to put our reason to the test.

Where does folklore intrude in our contemporary digital lives? Consider this: a short story about a fictional character, *The Slender Man*, became an internet phenomena, spawning stories, artwork, and even alleged photographs—despite being completely fictional. In May of 2014, two young girls stabbed a twelve-year-old classmate nineteen times, and when questioned, claimed they were acting as the Slender Man's proxies.

In a world where such fantasies can flourish, can any of us truly ignore the legend of Sawney and his family?

Appendices

Appendix A

The Horrid Life of Sawney Bean. An atrocious Robber & Assassin. (Carlisle: Jollie and Sons) [eight pages].
The History of Sawney Beane and his Family: Robbers and Murders. (Aldermary Church Yard, London) [eight pages, five cuts].
The Life of Sawney Beane, The Man-Eater Who inhabited a Cave near the Sea-Side in the County of Galloway in Scotland, upwards of Twenty-Five Years. (Market-Place, Hull: Printed by J. Ferraby) [twenty-four pages].
The Life of Sawney Bean, The Man-Eater, Who inhabited a Cave near the Sea-Side in the Country of Galloway in Scotland upwards of Twenty-Five Years to Which is Added the Droll Jester, Or Laugh when you can. (Butchery, Hull: J. Ferraby, Printer) [twenty-three pages].

Appendix B

The History of Sawney Beane and his Family, robbers and murderers, etc. Author: Sawney Beane (Birmingham: S. & T. Martin, 1810).
The Atrocious Cruelties of that Scotch Murderer, Robber, and Cannibal Sawney Beane. To which is added, the History of the murder of Joan Norkott, etc. (History of Thomas Austin.) (London: G. Smeeton, c. 1830).
Johnson's Lives of Highwaymen, etc. Sawney Beane; or, the Highland murderer ... Together with the lives of the Golden Farmer, Dick Walton ... and Tom Gerrard. (London, 1825).
The Lives and Adventures of Jack Shepherd, D. Morris, W. Nevison, and S. Beane; notorious thieves and highwaymen. (Manchester, 1839).
The life of Richard Turpin, a notorious highwayman. Containing a

particular account of his adventures, from his being first an apprentice to a butcher in Whitechapel, to his execution at York for horse-stealing. To which is added, the life of Sawney Beane, the man-eater. (London: printed by T. Maiden, for Ann Lemoine, and sold by T. Hurst, 1800).

Appendix C

Sawney Beane—S. & T. Martin, Printers Version

The
History of
Sawney Beane
And
His Family,
Robbers and Murderers,

Who took up their abode in a Cave, near the sea-side, where they lived twenty-five years, without going once to visit any City, Town or Village. The Robbed and Murdered about One Thousand Persons, whom they eat, but at last were happily discovered by a Pack of Bloodhounds; when SAWNEY BEANE, his Wife, Eight Sons, Six Daughters, Eight Grand Sons, and Fourteen Grand Daughters, were all seiz'd and Executed, in the manner here after specified.

Price One Penny

S. & T. Martin, Printers, Birmingham

The
History of
SAWNEY BEANE.

The following account, (tho as well attested as any historical fact can be) is almost incredible, for the monstrous and unparalleled barbarities that it relates; there being nothing that we ever heard of with the same degree of certainty that may be compared with it or that shows how far a brutish temper, untamed by education or knowledge of the world, may carry a man in such a glaring and horrible colours.

  Sawney Beane was born in the country of East Lothian, about eight or nine miles eastward of the city of Edinburgh, some time in the reign of Queen Elizabeth, whist King James I. governed Scotland. His parents worked at hedging and ditching for their livelihood, and brought up their Son by that occupation. He got his daily bread in his youth by that means: but being very much addicted to idleness and not chusing to be confined to any honest employment, he left his father and mother and ran away into the desert part of the country, taking with him a woman as viciously inclined as himself. These two took up their habitation in a rock by the sea-side on the shore of the country of Oalgay, where they lived upward of 25 years, without going into any city, town, or village.

In this time they had a great number of children and grand-children, whom they brought up after their own manner, without the least notion of humanity or of civil society. They never kept any company but among themselves and supported themselves by robbing; being moreover so very cruel, that they never robbed any body whom they did not murder.

By this bloody method, and their living so retiredly from the world they continued a long time undiscovered, there being nobody able to guess how the people were lost, who went by the place where they lived. As soon as they had robbed any one, they used to carry off their carcases to their den, where cutting them into quarters they would pickle the mangled limbs, and afterwards eat them, these being their only subsistence.

The people in the adjacent parts were alarmed at so uncommon a loss of their neighbours; for their was not travelling safely near the den of those wretches: this occasioned fresh spies in these parts, many of whom never returned again and those who did after the strictest search and enquiry, could not find how these melancholy matters happened.

There were several honest travellers taken up on suspicion and wrongfully hanged; several honest inn-keepers executed for no other reason than that the persons who had been thus lost, where known to have lain in their houses; which occasioned a suspicion of their being murdered by them, and their bodies privately buried in obscure places, to prevent a discovery. Thus an ill placed justice was executed with the greatest severity imaginable, to prevent their frequent atrocious deeds; so that not a few inn-keepers who lived on the western road in Scotland left off their business, for fear of being made examples of, and followed other employments. This, on the other hand, occasioned many inconveniences to passengers who were now in great distress for want of accommodation for themselves and horses, when they were disposed to bait or put up for lodging at night: In a word the whole country was almost depopulated.

Sawney's family was now grown very large; and every branch as soon as able, assisted in perpetrating their wicked deeds, which they followed with impunity; sometimes they would attack four, five, or six footmen together; but never more than two if on horseback.

They were also very careful that not one on whom the set upon, made their escape, am ambuscade being on every side, to secure the min every way. How then was it possible that they should be detected, when no one that saw them ever perceived any body afterwards?

The place they inhabited was solitary and lonesome; and when the tide came up, it went near two Hundred miles under ground: so that when some have been sent armed, they have passed by the mouth of the cave without any notice; not supposing that a human creature could reside in such a place of horror.

The number of people they destroyed was never exactly know; but it was computed that in twenty-five years they had murdered at least one thousand men, women, and children. The manner they were at last discovered was as follows:

A man and his wife behind him on the same horse, coming one evening home from a fair, and falling into an ambuscade of these merciless wretches, they attacked them in a very furious manner, the man to save himself fought bravely, riding some of them down by main force; but in the contest the poor women fell from behind him, and was instantly murdered before his face; the female cannibals, cutting her throat and sucking her blood with as great a gust as though it had been wine, this done, they ripped her up and pulled out her entrails; which dismal sight caused the man to make more resistance. It pleased providence while he was engaged, twenty or thirty came together in a body, on which Sawney Beane and his blood thirsty crew withdrew, and made the best of their way through a thick wood to their den.

This man was the first that ever fell in their way, that came off alive; he told the company what had happened, and showed them the body of his mangled wife, which the murderers had dragged out of the road, but had no time to carry off. They were struck with amazement, and went immediately to the Provost in Glasgow, who immediately sent to the King.

In a few days his Majesty in person, with a body of about four hundred men, set out for the place where these tragedies were acted in order to find out this hellish crew, which had so long been a nuisance to that part of the kingdom.

The man who had been attacked was the guide, and care was taken to have a vast number of blood-hounds, that no possible means might be wanting to put an end to these barbarous cruelties.

No sign of humanity was found for a long time; and even when they came to the cave of those wretches, they took not notice of it, but were going to pursue their search along the shore, the tide being then out; but some of the blood hounds luckily entered into this cave, and set up such a hideous barking, howling and yelping, that the King and his attendants came back and looked into it but did not think that any thing human could there be concealed. Nevertheless as the blood hounds went farther in, they increased their noise, and refused to come back; torches were then immediately ordered, and a great man men entered thro' the most intricate windings, til they came to the private recess of the murderers.

The whole body then went in, and saw the dismal sight, and were ready to sink into the earth to see such a number of arms, legs, thighs, hands, and feet of men, women, and children, hung up in rows like dry'd beef, and a great many lying in pickle. They also found a quantity of money, watches, rings swords, pistols, a large quantity of clothes, and other things which they had taken from those they murdered.

Sawney's family at this time consisted of himself his wife, eight sons, six daughters, eighteen grand-sons, and fourteen grand-daughters begotten in incest.

They were all seiz'd and pin-iron'd; and then they took what human flesh they found and buried in the sands; and taking all the spoils, the returned to Edinburgh, with the prisoners, the country flocking round to see this cursed tribe. When they came to Edinburgh, they were all committed to the Tolbooth, and the next day conducted under a strong guard to Leith, where they was all executed without any process, it being needless to try such creatures who were such professed enemies to mankind.

The men had first their privy members cut off, and thrown into the fire before their faces; then their hands and legs were cut off, by which amputation they bled to death in a few hours after.

The wife, daughters, and grand-children, having been made spectators of this just punishment inflected on the men, were burnt to death in three several fires. They all died without the least sign of repentance, and continued venting the most horrid imprecation to the last gasp of life.

FINIS.

Appendix D

The Tyburn Calendar, or Malefactors Bloody Register (G. Swindell, 1705).
A Compleat History of the Lives and Robberies of the Most Notorious Highwaymen, Foot-Pads, Shop-Lifts and Cheats of both sexes, in and about London and Westminster, and all parts of Great Britain, for above an hundred years past, continued to the present time by Captain Alexander Smith (1719).
The Chronicle of Tyburn, or Villainy Display'd in all its Branches (1720).
A General and True History of the Lives and Adventures of the Most

Famous Highwaymen, Murderers, Street-Robbers etc. To which is added a genuine Account of the Voyages and Plunders of the Most Noted Pirates, Interspersed with several remarkable Tryals of the most Notorious Malefactors, at the Sessions-House in the Old Bailey, London by Captain Charles Johnson (1734).

Lives of the most remarkable criminals condemned and executed for Murder, Highway Robberies, Housebreaking, Street Robberies and other Offences by John Osborn (1735)

The Tyburn Chronicle (1768).

The Newgate Calendar or MALEFACTORS' BLOODY REGISTER *containing: Genuine and Circumstantial Narrative of the lives and transactions, various exploits and Dying Speeches of the Most Notorious Criminals of both sexes who suffered Death Punishment in Gt. Britain and Ireland for High Treason Petty Treason Murder Piracy Felony Thieving Highway Robberies Forgery Rapes Bigamy Burglaries Riots and various other horrid crimes and misdemeanours on a plain entirely new, wherein will be fully displayed the regular progress from virtue to vice interspersed with striking reflexions on the conduct of those unhappy wretches who have fallen a sacrifice to the laws of their country.* (3 vols., 1774-1778) [N.B. This is the most commonly attributed title associated with *The Newgate Calendars*].

THE MALEFACTOR'S REGISTER; OR, *New* NEWGATE *and* TYBURN CALENDAR. CONTAINING THE AUTHENTIC LIVES, TRIALS, ACCOUNTS OF EXECUTIONS, DYING SPEECHES, AND OTHER CURIOUS PARTICULARS, *Relating to* ALL *the most notorious* VIOLATERS OF THE LAWS OF THEIR COUNTRY; WHO HAVE *Suffered* DEATH, *and other exemplary* PUNISHMENTS, *in England, Scotland, and Ireland, from the commencement of the Year 1700, to the* MIDSUMMER SESSIONS *of next Year. Together with* NUMEROUS TRIALS *in* EXTRAORDINARY CASES, *where the Parties have been* ACQUITTED. *This Work also comprehends all the most material Passages in the* SESSIONS-PAPERS *for a long Series of Years, and complete* NARRATIVES *of all the Capital* TRIALS *for* BIGAMY, HIGH-TREASON, RIOTS, BURGLARY, HORSE-STEALING, STREETROBBERY, FELONY, MURDER UNNATURAL CRIMES, FORGERY, PETIT-TREASON, FOOTPAD-ROBBERY, PIRACY, HIGHWAY-ROBBERY, RAPES, *And various other* OFFENCES, *and* MISDEMEANORS. *To which is added, A correct List of all the Capital Convictions at the Old Bailey, etc. etc. etc. since the Commencement of the present Century; which will be of the highest Use to refer to on many Occasions. The Whole tending, by a general Display of the Progress and Consequence of Vice, to impress on the Mind proper Ideas* of the Happiness resulting from a Life of strict Honor and Integrity: and to convince Individuals of the superior Excellence of those Laws framed for the Protection of our Lives and Properties. Offered not only as an Object of Curiosity and Entertainment, but as a Work of real and substantial Use. Dedicated to Sir JOHN FIELDING, Knight (1780).

The Criminal Recorder (1804).

The New and Complete Newgate Calendar or Malefactor's Universal Register, Comprising INTERESTING MEMOIRS of the MOST NOTORIOUS CHARACTERS who have been convicted of outrages on the LAWS OF ENGLAND, with SPEECHES, CONFESSIONS, and LAST EXCLAMATIONS of SUFFERERS by William Jackson (1818).

The Newgate Calendar Improved; Being interesting memoirs of notorious characters who have been convicted of Offence against the laws of England, During the seventeenth century; and continued to the present time, chronologically arranged; comprising Traitors, Murderers, Incendiaries, Ravishers, Pirates, Mutineers, Coiners, Highwaymen, Footpads, Housebreakers, Rioters, Extortioners, Sharpers, Forgers, Pickpockets, Fraudulent Bankrupts, Money droppers, Impostors, and Thieves of every Description. And Containing a number of interesting cases never before published: with Occasional remarks on Crimes and Punishments, Original Anecdotes, Moral reflections and Observations on particular Cases; Explanations of the Criminal Laws, the Speeches, Confessions and Last Exclamations of Sufferers. To which is added a Correct Account of the Various Modes of Punishment of criminals in Different Parts of the World by George Theodore Wilkinson, esq. (1822).

Celebrated Trials, and remarkable cases of Criminal Jurisprudence from the earliest Records to the Year 1825 by George Borrow (1825).

The Newgate Calendar by Andrew Knapp and William Baldwin (1826).

The Chronicles of Crime or the New Newgate Calendar, being a series of memoirs and anecdotes of notorious characters who have outraged the laws of Great Britain from the earliest period to 1841 by Camden Pelham (1841, reprinted 1886).

The Terrific Register—or Record of Crimes, Judgments, Providences and Calamities, vol I. (1825).

Appendix E

Nicholson, John, *Historical and Traditional Tales in Prose and Verse, Connected With The South of Scotland.* (Kirkcudbright: John Nicholson, 1843) p. 72-80.

Sawney Bean and his Family

The following account, though as well attested as any historical fact can be, is almost incredible for the monstrous and unparalleled barbarities that it relates; there being nothing that we ever heard of, with the same degree of certainty, that might be compared with it, or shews how far a brutal temper, untamed by education and knowledge of the world, may carry a man in such glaring and horrible colours.

Sawney Bean was born in the county of East Lothian, about eight or nine miles eastward of the city of Edinburgh, in the reign of James I. of Scotland. His father was a hedger and ditcher and brought up his sons to the same laborious employment.

He got his daily bread in his youth by these means, but being very prone to idleness, and not caring to be confined to any honest employment, he left his father and mother, and ran way into the desert part of the country, taking with him a woman as viciously inclined as himself.

These two took up their habitation in a cave, but the sea-side on the shore of the county of Galloway; where they lived upwards of twenty-five years, without going into any city, town or village.

In this time they had a great number of children and grandchildren, whom they brought up after their own manner, without any notion of humanity or civil society—They never kept any company but among themselves, and supported themselves wholly by robbing: being, moreover so very cruel, that they never robbed any one, whom they did not murder.

By this bloody method, and their being so retired from the world, they continued for a long time undiscovered: there being no person able to guess how the people were lost that went by the place where they lived. As soon as they had robbed any man, woman or child, they used to carry off the carcase to the den where cutting it into quarters, they would pickle the mangled limbs, and afterwards eat it; this being their only sustenance: and not withstanding they were at last so numerous, they commonly had superfluity of this their abominable food, so that in the night-time they frequently threw legs and arms of the un-happy wretches they had murdered into the sea, at a great distance from their bloody habitation: the limbs were often cast up by the tide in several parts of the country, to the astonishment and terror of all beholders and others who heard of it.

Persons who have gone about their lawful occasions fell so often into their hands, that it caused a general outcry in the country round about: no person knowing what was become of their friends or relations, if they were once seen by these merciless cannibals.

All the people in the adjacent parts were at least alarmed at such an uncommon loss of their neighbours and acquaintance, for there was no travelling in safety near the den of theirs wretches: this occasioned spies to be frequently sent into those parts, many of whom never returned again, and those who did, after the strictest search and inquiry, could not find how these melancholy matters happened.

Several honest travellers were taken up on suspicion and wrongfully hanged upon bare circumstances: several innocent inn keepers were executed, for no other reason than that persons, who had thus been lost, where known to have lain in their houses, which occasioned a suspicion of their being murdered by them and their bodies privately buried in obscure paces to prevent a discovery. Thus an ill-placed justice was executed with the greatest severity imaginable, in order to prevent these frequent, atrocious deeds: so many innkeepers, who lived on the western road of Scotland, left their business, for fear of being made examples of, and followed other employments.

This, on the other hand, occasioned many inconveniences to travellers, who were no in great distress for accommodation when they were disposed to refresh themselves and horses, or take up lodging for the night. In a word, the whole country was almost depopulated.

Still the king's subjects were as much missed as before, so it became the admiration of the whole kingdom how such villainies could be carried on, and the perpetrators not discovered. A great many had been executed, not one of them made any confession at the gallows, but maintained to last that they were perfectly innocent of the crime for which they suffered.

When the magistrates found all was in vain, they left off these rigorous proceedings, and trusted wholly to Providence, for the bringing to light the authors of these unparalleled barbarities when it should seem proper to the divine wisdom.

Sawney's family was at last grown very large and every branch of it soon as able, assisted in the perpetrating their wicked deeds, which they still followed with impunity—Sometimes they would attack four, five or six, footmen together, but never more than two, if they were on horseback; they were, moreover, so careful that not one whom they had set upon should escape, that an ambuscade was set on every side to secure them, let them fly which way they would, provided it should ever happen that one or more got away from the first assailants. How was it possible they should be detected, when not one that ever saw any body else afterwards.

The place which they inhabited was quite solitary and lonesome, and, when the time came up, the water went near two hundred yards into their subterraneous habitation, which reached almost a mile underground; so that when people, who had been sent armed to search all the places about, have passed by the mouth of the cave, they have never taken any notice of it, never supposing any human being would reside in such a place of perpetual horror and darkness.

The number of people these savages destroyed was never exactly known; but it was generally computed that in the twenty-five years they continued their butcheries, they had washed their hands with the blood of at least a thousand men, women and children. The manner they were at last discovered was as follows—

A man and his wife behind him on the same horse, coming one evening home from a fair, and falling into the ambuscade of these merciless wretches, they fell upon them in a furious manner. The man to save himself as well as he could, fought very bravely against them with sword and pistol, riding some of them down by main force of his horse.

In the conflict the poor woman fell from behind him, and was instantly butchered before her husband's face, for the female cannibals cut her throat and fell to sucking her blood with great a gust, as if it had been wine: this done, they ript up her belly, and pulled out all her entrails. Such a dreadful spectacle made the man make more obstinate resistance, as he expected the same fate, if he fell into their hands.

It pleased Providence while he was engaged that twenty or thirty who had been at the same fair, came together in a body, upon which Sawney Bean and his blood thirsty clan withdrew and, made the best of their way through a thick wood to their den.

This man who was the first who had ever fell in their way, and came off alive, told the whole company what had happened, and shewed them the horrid spectacle of his wife, whom the murderers had dragged to same distance, but had not time to carry her entirely off. They were all struck with stupefaction and amazement at what he related; they took him with them to Glasgow, and told the affair to the magistrates of that city, who immediately sent to the king concerning it.

In about three or four days after, his majesty in person, with a body of about four hundred men, set out for the place where this dismal tragedy was acted, in order to search all of the rocks and thickets, that, if possible, they might apprehend this hellish crew, which had so long pernicious been to all western parts of the kingdom.

The man who was attacked was the guide, and care was taken to have a large number of blood-hounds with them, that no human means might be wanting towards their putting an entire end to these cruelties.

No sign of any habitation was to be found for a long time; and even when they came to the wretches' cave, they took no notice of it, but were going to pursue their search along the sea shore, the tide being taken out; but some of the blood-hounds luckily entered the Cimmerian den, and instantly set up a most hideous barking, howling and yelping; so that the king, with his attendants, came back, and looked into it: they could not tell how to conceive that any human being could be concealed in a place where they saw nothing but darkness; but nevertheless, as the blood hounds increased their noise they went further in, and refused to come back again, they then began to imagine something or other must inhabit there. Torches were immediately sent for, and a great many men ventured in, through the most intricate turnings and windings, till at last they arrived at that private recess from all the world, which was the habitation of these monsters.

Now the whole body, or as many of them as could went in, and were all so shocked at what they beheld, that they were almost ready to sink into the earth. Legs, arms, thighs, hands, and feet of men, women and children, were hung up in rows like dried beef; a great many limbs laid in pickle, and a great mass of money both gold and silver, with watches, rings, swords, pistols and a large quantity of cloaths, both linen and woollen, and an infinite number of other things which they had taken from those they had murdered, where thrown together in heaps or hung up against the sides of the den.

Sawney's family, at this time, besides himself, consisted of his wife, eight sons, six daughters, eighteen grand sons, and fourteen grand-daughters, where were all begotten in incest.

These were all seized and pinioned by his majesty's order in the first place; then they took what human flesh they could find, and buried it in the sands; afterwards loading themselves with the spoils which they found, they returned to Edinburgh with their prisoners; all the country, as they passed along, flocked to see this cursed tribe. When they came to their journey's end, the wretches were committed to the Tolbooth, from whence they were the next day conducted, under a strong guard, to Leith, where they were executed without any process, it being thought needless to try creatures who were ever professed enemies to mankind.

The men were dismembered, their hands and legs severed from their bodies by which amputation they bled to death in a few hours. The wife, daughters, and grand-children, having been made spectators of this just punishment inflicted on the man, were afterwards burnt to death in three several fires. They all in general died without the last signs of repentance, but continued cursing and vending the most dreadful imprecations to the very last gasp.

Appendix F

Crockett, Samuel Rutherford, *The Grey Man* (Ayr: Macdonald and Sprout, 1977), pp. 242-246.

Then the horrid brabblement filled all the cave, and sounded louder and more outrageous, being heard in darkness. Suddenly, however, the murky gloom was shot through with beams of light, and a rout of savages, wild and bloody, filled the wide cave beneath us. Some of them carried crude torches, and others had various sorts of backburdens, which they cast down in the corners. I gat a gliff of one of these, and though in battle I had often seen things grim and butcherly, my heart now sprang to my mouth, so that I had well-nigh fainted with loathing. But I commanded myself, and thrust me before Hell, who from where she sat could only see the flickering skarrow of the torches upon the roof and walls—for the place seemed now, after the former darkness of Egypt, fairly bursting with light.

Then I knew that these execrable hell-hounds must be the hideous crew who called Sawny Bean lord and master. They were of both sexes and all ages, mostly running naked, the more stalwart of them armed with knives and whingers, or with knotted piece of tree in which a ragged stone had been thrust and tied with sinew or tags of rope. The very tottering children were striking at one another, or biting like young wolves, till the blood flowed. In the corner sat an old bleared hag, who seemed of some authority over them, for she pointed with her finger, and the uproar calmed a little. The shameless naked women-crew began to bestir themselves, and heaped broken driftwood upon the floor, to which presently a light was set.

Then the red climbing flame went upward. The wood smoke filled the cave, acrid and tickling, which getting into our throats, might have worked us infinite danger, had it not been that the clamour of the savages was so great that it never stilled for a moment. But in time we became accustomed to the reek, and it disturbed us not.

More by luck than good guiding, the place where we sat was, as I have said, favourably situated for the seeing without being seen—being a kind of natural balcony or chamber in a wall, like a swallow's nest plastered under the eaves of a barn. We learned afterwards that it was a place forbidden by Sawny Bean, the head of the clan, and so kept sacred for himself when it should please him to retire thither for his ease and pleasure, with whomsoever he would of his unholy crew. And to this no doubt we owed our safety, for the young impish boys roamed everywhere else, specially swarming and yelling about our boat, which they had just discovered. I noted, also, that when any of these came in the way of the men, he was knocked down incontinent with a hand, a knife, or a stick, as was the most convenient. Sometimes the lad would lie a minute or two where he had been struck, then up again, and to the playing and disport he fell, as though nothing had happened at all.

All this was horrid enough, but that was not the worst of it, and I own that I hesitate to write that which I saw. Yet, for the sake of the truth, tell I must and will. The cavern was very high in the midst, but at the sides not so high—rather like the sloping roof of an attic, which slants quickly down from the rooftree. But that which took my eye amid the smoke were certain vague shapes, as it had been of the limbs of human beings, shrunk and blackened, which hung in rows on either side of the cave. At first it seemed that my eyes must certainly deceive me, for the reek drifted hither and thither, and made the rheum flow from them with its bitterness. But after a little study of these wall adornments, I could make nothing else of it, than that these poor relics, which hung in rows from the roof of the cave like hams and black puddings set to dry in the smoke, where indeed no other than the parched arms and legs of men and women who had once walked the upper earth—but who by misfortune had fallen into the power of this hideous, inconceivable gang of monstrous maneaters. Then the rue interpretation of all the tales that went floating about the countryside, and which I had hitherto deemed wholly vain and fantastical, burst upon me. [...]

[pp. 249-251]

The water-door of the cave was now entirely filled with a black hulk, in shape like a grizzly ape. Even in the flickering light I knew instantly that I had seen the monster before. A thrill ran through me when I remembered the man-beast, the thing with which I had grappled in the barn of Culzean the night I out-faced the Grey Man. And now, by the silence and the crouching of the horde beneath me, I learned that their master had come home. The monster stood a moment in the doorway as though angered at something, then he spoke in a voice like a beast's growl, certain things which I could not at all understand—though it was clear that his progeny did, for there ensued a tumultuous rushing from side to side. Then Sawny Bean strode into the midst of his den. It happened that by misadventure he stumbled and set his foot upon a lad of six or seven, judging by the size of him, who sprawled naked in the doorway. The imp squirmed round like a serpent and bit Sawny Bean in the leg, whereat he stooped, and catching the lad by the feet, he dashed his head with a dull crash against the wall, and threw him quivering like a dead rabbit into the corner.

The rest stood for a moment aghast. But in a trice, and without a single one so much as going to see if the boy were dead or only stunned, the whole hornet's byke hummed again, and the place was filled with a stifling smell of burning fat and roasting victual, upon the origin of which I dared not let my mind for a moment dwell.

When Sawny Bean came in, he had that which looked like a rich cloth of god over his arm—the plunder of some poor butchered wretch, belike. He stood with this trophy in front of him, examining it before the fire. Presently he threw it over his shoulders, with the arms hanging idly down in front, and strode about most like a play-actor or a mad person—but manifestly to his own great content and to the huge admiration of his followers, who stood still and gaped after him.

When he had satisfied himself with this posturing, the monster looked towards our place of refuge. A great spasm seized my heart when I saw him take the first step towards us, for I guess that it was his forbidden treasure-house in which we lurked.

So I thought it had certainly come to the last bitter push with us. But something yet more terrible than the matter of the boy diverted us for the moment the monster's attention. The lad whom he had cast to the side had been left alone, none daring to meddle. But now, as he passed him, Sawny Bean gave the body a toss with his foot. At this, quick as a darting falcon on the stoop, a woman sprang at him from a crevice where she had been couching—at least by her shape she was a woman, with long elflocks twisting like snakes about her brow and over her shoulders. She held an open knife in her hand, and she struck at the chieftan's hairy breast. I heard the point strike the flesh, and the cry of anger and pain which followed. But the monster caught the woman by the wrist, pulled her over his knee, and bent back her head. It was a horrid thing to see, and there is small wonder that I can see it yet in many a dream of the night. And no doubt also I shall see it till I die—hear it as well, which is worse.

Then for a long season I could look no more. But when I had recovered me a little, and could again command my heart, I saw a great part of the crew swarm thick as flies—fetching, carrying and working like bees upon spilled honey about the corner where had lain the bodies of the lad and the woman. But it was not in the ordinary way that these were being prepared for burial. In the centre of the cave sat Sawny Bean, with some of the younger sort of the women pawing over him and bandaging his wounded shoulder. He was growling and spitting inarticulately all the while like a wild cat. And every time his shoulder hurt him as the women worked with the wound and mouthed it, he would take his other hand and strike one of them down, as though it was to her that he owned the twinge of pain.

Presently the monster arose and took the gold brocade again in his hand. I thought that of certainty now our time was come, and I looked at Nell Kennedy.

God knows what was in my eyes. My heart within me was ready to break, for the like of this pass had never man been in. That I should have to smite my love to the death within an hour of my first kiss and the first owning of her affection.

But she that loved me read my thought in mine eyes.

She bared her neck for me, so that I could see its tender whiteness in the flicker of the fire.

'Strike there,' she said 'and let me die in your arms who art my own hart's love, Launcelot Kennedy.'

I heard the beast-man's step on the stair. I looked form Nell's dear neck to her eyes and back again to her bosom. Then I lifted my hand with the steel in it, and nerved myself for the striking, for I must make no mistake. And even in that moment I saw the gleam of a dagger in Marjorie's hand also.

Suddenly a tremendous rush of sound filled the cave. The blade fell from my hand, and by instinct, not knowing what we did, Nell and I clasped one another. The clamour seemed to be all about us and all round us. Roaring echoes came back to us. The bowels of the earth quaked. Yet methought there was something strongly familiar in the sound of it. I turned me about and there, standing erect with all his little height was the Dominie. His cheeks were distended, and he was blowing upon his great war-pipes such a thunderous pibroch as never had been heard east of the Minch since the island pipes skirled on the Red Harlaw.

What madcap possession had come upon his mind, I know not . But the effect I can tell. The pack of fiends that caroused and slew beneath, stood stricken a moment in amaze at the dreadful incomprehensible sounds. Then they fled helter-skelter, yellyhooing with fear, down the narrow sea-way from which the tide had now fully ebbed. And when I looked again, there was not a soul to be seen. Only over the edge of a lappered cauldron the body of the murdered (or, at least, a part of it), lay doubled—a bloody incentive to make haste out of this direful Cave of Death. [...]

[pp. 277-281: Launcelot returns to the Beans' cave with the king, in pursuit of John Mure.]

Then I knew that I was lost indeed. For by the flickering light of the dying fire of driftwood I could see I was again in the cave of Sawny Bean, in the same wide hall with the strange narrow hams a-swing on the roof, the tubs of salt meat festering under the eaves, and the wild savage crew dancing about me.

What wonder that my heart fainted within me to be thus left alone in that den of hideous things, and especially to think of the free birds going to their beds on the cliffs above me and the fishing solan geese circling and balancing home to the lonely rock of Ailsa.

'Ha, Sir Launcelot Kennedy,' said a mocking voice as the deafening turmoil quieted a little, 'you are near your honours now—that is, if there be such bauble dignities either in heaven or hell. The Treasure of Kelwood in hand, John Mure's life out of hand—and there on the shelf (as it were) are your broad acres and your boony lady!'

I was silent, for I knew that nothing could avail me now. It was useless to waste words.

'But ere all that comes to pass,' he went on, 'there are sundry little formalities to be gone through.—Oh, we are right dainty folk here in Sawny Bean's mansion. You shall be kept warm and cherished tenderly. There are here twenty sonsier queans than the one whose heart you desire. Warmly shall they welcome, sweetly shall they cherish handsome Sir Launcelot. Their embracements shall sting you more than all sweetheartening raptures.'

Again he pauses to observe the effect of his [John Mure's] words.

'You that so lately held me in chase like a steer that has escaped from the shambles. Now you yourself are in the thills. You that have crossed me a thousand times in my plans since that frore night in Sir Thomas Nesbitt's yard in Maybole, you shall now be crossed in a new fashion. You that wagged tongue some merrily at another's expense, you shall see your tongue wag the redhot brander to an unkenned tune.

'You have ridden so fast and so far, you shall ride your last ride—ride slowly, very slowly,' cried the fiend in my ear, 'for I shall hoard every drop of your blood as John of Cassillis hoards his gold rose nobles. I shall husband every minute of your life, as though there were the hours of young bridal content.

'Ye have bruised my old face indeed with your oaken staff, but I will cherish ours, that is youthful and blooming. Tenderly shall we take off that coverture of hide, the tegument of beauty. Sawny Bean has famous skill in such surgery. Gently will we lay you down in the swarming nest of the patient ant. We have read how Scriptures bids the sluggard to go to the ant, for that makes him not lively, nothing will. I have ofttimes commented on the passage at family worship. And I must see that the young and headstrong, like you, my Lord Launcelot, give heed to that which is commended.'

But in spite of all this terrible threatening, I bode still and answered him never a word. They laid logs of driftwood upon the fire, till the whole inside of the cave grew bright and clear; and all monstrous deformity of the women and the cruel hideousness of the men were made apparent as in broad daylight. Some of them were painted and stained like demons, and danced and leaped through the fire like them, too. For such monsters have not been heard of, much less seen, in the history of any country as were Sawny Bean and his crew in the cave upon the seashore of Bennanbrack.

'Bring me a knife,' cried John Mure from where he sat, for he appeared like a chief devil among a company of gibbering lubber fiends. He had still his grey cloak about him. His plumed hat was upon his head, and he looked, save for the eyes of him in which the fires of hell burned, a civil, respectable, well-put-on man of means and substance. As, indeed, save for his evil heart, he might have been, for he came from as good a family as the Earl of Cassillis, or, as it might be, as I myself, Launcelot Kennedy of Kirrieoch.

So when Auchendrayne asked for a knife, Sawny Bean himself, the ruffian kemper, low-browed, buck-toothed, and inhuman, brought it to him with a grin. He made as if he would have set it in me to the hilt. But John Mure stayed him.

'Bide,' he said, 'not so fast. There is long and sweet pleasuring to come before that—such slow, relishing delight, such covetous mouseplay of the brindled cat, such luxurious tiger-licking of the delicate skin till it be raw, such well-conceited dainty torments as when one would bite his love and be glad of it. He shall taste them all, this frolic squire of errant-dames, this gamesome player upon pipes, this curious handler of quant love tunes. Ere we pluck the red rose of his life, he shall sate himself with new delicious experience—rarer than the handling of many maidens' tresses.'

I was moved to speak to him.

'I ask not mercy,' said I, 'for I own that I would have killed you if I could. But you are a valiant man, give me a sword and let me make a stand for it against you all, that as I have lived so I may also die fighting.'

'If I be a man, as you say—who said that I was a man? Do I act as other men? Is my knowledge like that of other men? Do I company with other men? Call that a man? (He pointed to Sawny Bean, who for wantonness sat on an upturned tub, striking with a keen-edged knife at the legs of all that came by for mere delight of blood, storming at them meantime with horrid imprecations to approach nearer and be flicked.) Or call these men? (He showed me some of the younger cannibal race gnawing like kenneled dogs at horrid bones.) Nay, my dainty wanton, you shall not enter Hell through the brave brattle of warring blades, nor yet handling your rapier like a morris-dancer. But as the blood drains from to the white from the stricken calf, so shall they whiten your flesh for the tooth, and so reluctantly shall your life drop from you drop by drop.'

And I declare that this scornful fiend telling me of tortures in choice words made me scunner more than the prick of the knife. For the abhorred invention quickened the imagination and set the nerves agate.

So that I was honestly glad when he took the knife in hand—a shoemaker's curved blade with a keen cutting edge.

'Strip him naked!' he cried. And very cheerfully so they did, smiting me the meantime with the broad of their hand.

Then John Mure leaned over me delicately, and made as though he would have traced with his knife the jointing of my limbs, saying 'Thus and thus shall the she-tribe dismember your body when the torture of the ant's nest is ended.' And again 'Here is toothsome eating, Sawny Bean, thou chief lover of dainty vivers.'

Then, as the evil man went on with his pitiless jestings, his grey cloak began to waver before me, his face to glow like fire, and I fainted or dwamed away till the sharp knife pricked me into consciousness again.

Yet Auchendrayne overdid his threatening, for the too sharp relish of the words issued entranced dullness ere the matter came to action. And of torture there was none that I can now remember or bear the mark of—save only the slight scores of the knife which he made when he showed me where they would joint and haggle my body.

Indeed, I mind no more till I came to myself, lying on my back, with the cave all empty save for John Mure—who sat, as before, with his hand to his ear listening.

But there sounded a great and furious uproar down by the cave mouth, the deep baying of bloodhounds, the fierce cry of many voices striving for mastery, and above all the shrieks of the smitten.

Surely I thought, there is a battle fierce and fell at the cave's mouth. John Mure sat and listened for a long space and presently he looked over me.

'I will even make sure of him, come what may,' he said.

And with that he took the knife and came nearer to smite me in the breast, and I lay as one dead already, waiting for the stroke.

But even in that moment as I held my breath a ravening hound darted within the cave, overleaped the embers of the fire, and pinned the grey-haired murderer to the earth by the throat. He struck out desperately, but the dog held him fast. Another and another came in, till, as it seemed, he was in danger of being torn to pieces of dogs.

But me they minded not at all, for (as I say) I lay as one dead.

Endnotes

Prologue

1. 'Sawney just loved baked human beans', *The Sun* (12 September 1994), p. 4.

Chapter One

1. Tolkien, J. R. R., *The Fellowship of the Ring* (New York: Ballantine Books, 1976), p. 241.

Chapter Two

1. Timothy Taylor, 'The Edible Dead', *British Archeology*, 59, June 2001 (http://www.archaeologyuk.org/ba/ba59/feat1.shtml).
2. Maxwell, Sir Herbert, *A History of Dumfries and Galloway* (Edinburgh: William Blackwood and Sons, 1896) pp. 3-4.
3. *ibid.*, pp. 16-18.
4. *ibid.*, pp. 23-24.
5. *ibid.*, p. 32.
6. Mackenzie, William, *History of Galloway From the Earliest Time to the Present*, vol. 1 (Kirkcudbright: John Nicholson, 1841), pp. 48-60.
7. *ibid.*
8. Macleod, Innes F, *Where the Whaups Are Crying: A Dumfries and Galloway Anthology* (Glasgow: Birlinn, 2001), p. 41.
9. Fiona Armstrong, 'Dumfries & Galloway', *Scotland Magazine*, 2, June 2002, p. 46.
10. Nicholson, John, *Historical and Traditional Tales in Prose and Verse Connected With the South of Scotland* (Kirkcudbright: John Nicholson, 1843), p. 39.
11. *ibid.*
12. *ibid.*, pp. 38-39.
13. *ibid.*, p. 39.
14. Armstrong, p. 46.

15. Doubleday, H. Arthur., *The Works of William Shakespeare* (London: Chiswick Press, 1896), p. 136.
16. Giles, J. A., *Matthew Paris's English History From 1235 to 1273, vol. 1* (London: Henry G. Bohn, 1852), pp. 30-42.
17. Armstrong, p. 46.
18. *ibid.*
19. McLachlan, Malcolm, *Rambles in Galloway: Topographical, and Biographical* (Edinburgh: Edmonston & Douglas, 1876), pp. 8-9.
20. *ibid.*, p. 9.
21. *ibid.*
22. Black, Ray, *Cannibals and Evil Cult Killers: The Most Unthinkable and Heinous Crimes* (London: Little Brown, 2006), p. 9.
23. Taylor.
24. McKie, Robin, 'Bones from a Cheddar Gorge cave show that cannibalism helped Britain's earliest settlers survive the ice age', 20 June 2010, (http://www.theguardian.com/science/2010/jun/20/ice-age-cannibals-britain-earliest-settlers).
25. *ibid.*
26. Black, Ray, *Cannibals and Evil Cult Killers: The Most Unthinkable and Heinous Crimes*, p. 10.
27. Jonathan Amos, 'Ancient Britons "drank from skulls"', 16 January 2011, (http://www.bbc.co.uk/news/science-environment-12478115).
28. P. H. M'Kerlie, R.S.A. SCOT., F.R.G.S., etc., *History of the Lands and Their Owners In Galloway With Historical Sketches of the District* (London: Simpkin, Marshall, Hamilton, Kent & Co. LMD) 1906, p. 31.
29. Buckle, Henry Thomas, *History of Civilisation in England*, vol. 2 (New York: D. Appleton, 1864), p. 135.
30. *ibid.*, p. 135.
31. Holinshed, Raphael, *Scottish Chronicle: A Complete History and Description of Scotland*, vol. 1 (Glasgow: A. Wilson, 1805), p. 16.
32. *ibid.*, pp. 16-17.
33. Roughead, William, *Rogues Walk Here (London: Cassell, 1934), pp. 92-93.*
34. George Gould MD and Walter L. Pyle, *Anomalies and Curiosities of Medicine* (Philadelphia: W. B. Saunders, 1900), p. 409.
35. Cheviot, Andrew, *Proverbs, Proverbial Expressions And Popular Rhymes Of Scotland* (Edinburgh: Alexander Gardner, 1896), p. 198.
36. Ashton, John, *Chap-Books of the Eighteenth Century* (Piccadilly: Chatto And Windus, 1882), p. vii.
37. *ibid.*, p. i.
38. *ibid.*, p. viii.
39. Harness, Reverend W. *Shakespeare's Dramatic Works,* Love's Labour Lost, Act II, Scene I (London: J. F. Dove, 1830), pp. 137.
40. R. S. Ferguson, 'On the Collection of Chap-books in the Bibliotheca Jacksoniana, in Tullie House, Carlisle, with some remarks on the History of Printing in Carlisle, Whitehaven, Penrith and other north country towns', *Transactions of the Cumberland and Westmoreland Antiquarian and Archeological Society*, 14 (1897), pp. 1-120.

41. Ashton, pp. vii-x.
42. David Cornwell and Sandy Hobbs, 'Sawney Bean, the Scottish Cannibal', *Folklore*, 108 (1997), pp. 49-50.
43. *ibid.*, p. 50.
44. BBC article 'The Grisly Deeds of Sawney Bean', March 2011 (http://www.bbc.co.uk/scotland/history/sawney_bean.shtml).
45. Johnson, Captain Charles, *A General and True History of the Lives and Actions Of the Most Famous Highwaymen, Murderers, Street-Robbers, &c. To Which is Added, A Genuine Account of the Voyages and Plunders, Of the Most Noted Pirates. Interspersed with several remarkable Tryals Of the Most Notorious Malefactors ... at the Sessions-House in the Old Baily, London. Adorn'd with the Effigies, and Other Material Transactions of the Most Remarkable Offenders, Engraved on Copper Plates* (Birmingham: R. L. Walker, 1742), pp. 31-33.

Chapter Three

1. Jackson, Henry, *Robinson Crusoe Social Engineer, How the discovery of Robinson Crusoe solves the labor problem and opens the path to industrial peace* (New York: E. P. Button and Company, 1922), p. 23.
2. Holmes, Ronald, *The Legend of Sawney Bean* (London: Mews, 1975), p. 129.
3. *ibid.*, p. 130.
4. Mackay, John, *Cannibal Family of Sawney Bean and Stories of South West Scotland* (Glasgow: Lang Syne, 2007), pp. 17-22.
5. Van der Kiste, John, *William and Mary* (London: The History Press, 2003), p. 255.
6. Mackenzie, Ross, *Culloden, The Swords and the Sorrows* (Glasgow: The National Trust for Scotland Trading Company, 1996), pp. 4-7.
7. *ibid.*, p. 8.
8. Chambers, Robert, *History of the Rebellion in Scotland in 1745, 1746* (London: W & R Chambers, 1869), p. 183.
9. Charles MacKay and Allan G. May Ramsay, *A Dictionary of Lowland Scotch* (Boston: Ticknor, 1888), p. 174.
10. Pittock, Murray G. H., *The Myth of the Jacobite Clans* (Edinburgh: Edinburgh University Press, 1999), pp. 9-10.
11. *The Official Scrabble Player's Dictionary*, 4th ed. (New York: Merriam-Webster, 2005), p. 536.
12. *Special Collections*, National Library of Scotland.
13. *ibid.*
14. *ibid.*
15. *The History of Sawney Beane and his Family, robbers and murderers, etc. Author: Sawney Beane* (Birmingham: S. & T. Martin, 1810), p. 3.
16. *Special Collections.*
17. *Special Collections.*
18. Peter Christie, 'The True Story of the North Devon Savages', *Transactions of the Devonshire Association*, 124, December 1992, p. 84.

19. McMahon, Vanessa, *Murder in Shakespeare's England* (London: Hambledon & London, 2004), pp. 223-32.
20. *ibid.*
21. Bernard Capp, 'Serial Killers in 17th-Century England', *HistoryToday*, 46.3 (1996), (http://www.historytoday.com/story/13835).

Chapter Four

1. *The Newgate Calendar*, vol. 1, ed. by Donal Ó Danachair (The Ex-Classics Project, 2009) (http://www.exclassics.com/newgate/ng01.pdf), p. 10.
2. *ibid.*, p. 1-4.
3. *ibid.*, p. 2.
4. Kerman, Sandra Lee, *The Newgate Calendar or Malefactor's Bloody Register* (New York: Capricorn, 1962), p. vi.
5. *ibid.*, p. xiii.
6. *ibid.*, pp. 42-46.
7. *The Terrific Register—or Record of Crimes, Judgments, Providences and Calamities, vol. 1* (London: Sherwood, Jones, and Co., 1825), pp. 164-166.

Chapter Five

1. MacDiarmid, Hugh, *The Scottish Eccentrics* (London: George Routledge & Sons, 1936), p. 185.
2. Cross, F. C., *Songs Duets and Choruses in the Semi-Comic Pantomime of Harlequinn Highlander, or Sawney Bean's Cave*, performed at the Jones's Royal Circus, 11 June 1798, from the National Library of Scotland.
3. *The London Quarterly Review*, October 1896-January 1897 (London: C. H. Kelly, 1897), p. 394.
4. Crockett, Samuel Rutherford, *The Grey Man* (Ayr: Macdonald and Sprout, 1977), p. 107.
5. *ibid.*, p. 134.
6. *ibid.*, p. 210.
7. *ibid.*, p. 212.
8. *ibid.*, p. 214.
9. *ibid.*, p. 242.
10. *ibid.*
11. Hamilton, Judy, *Scottish Murders* (New Lanark: Geddes & Grosset, 2001), pp. 17-24.

Chapter Six

1. Cornwell and Hobbs, p. 49.
2. Johnson, Captain Charles, p. 31.
3. Nicholson, p. 72.
4. Gribble, Leonard, *More Famous Historical Mysteries* (London: Frederick Muller, 1972), pp. 32-33.
5. Lang, Andrew W., *A Short History of Scotland* (London: Andrew Lang, 1911). p 39.

6. *ibid.*, p. 41.
7. *ibid.*, p. 97.
8. 'History of the "Silver Gun" and the Silver Arrow, and the winners of the trophies as extracted from Minute Books of the Six Incorporated Trades of the Town' (http://www.old-kirkcudbright.net/pages/siller.asp).
9. Lamont-Brown, Raymond, *Scottish Folklore* (Edinburgh: Birlinn, 1996), p. 86.
10. Robertson, William, *Historical Tales and Legends of Ayrshire* (London: Himilton, Adams and Co., 1889) and Agnew, Andrew, *The Hereditary Sheriffs of Galloway* (Edinburgh David Douglas, 1893).
11. Love, Dane, *Legendary Ayrshire, Custom, Folklore, Tradition* (Ayr: Carn, 2009), pp. 142-143.
12. *ibid.*
13. 'The Burning of the Ayr and Dairy Witches' (http://www.maybole.org/history/books/legends/burning.htm).
14. Wood, J. Maxwell, *Witchcraft in South-West Scotland* (Dumfries: EP, 1975), pp. 112-114.
15. *ibid.*, p. 113.
16. Roughead, p. 88.

Chapter Seven

1. Cornwell and Hobbs, p. 49.
2. Crockett, p. 134.
3. Interview of author Tom Barclay, Reference & Local History Librarian, South Ayrshire Libraries, May 2013.
4. *ibid.*
5. 'Sawney Bean: Myth or Myth', *Ayrshire Notes*, 23 (Autumn 2002), p. 16.
6. Lang, Theo, *The Queen's Scotland—Glasgow, Kyle and Galloway* (London: Hodder and Stoughton, 1953), pp. 129-130.
7. *Carricta Meridionalis Map of South Carrick*, South Ayshire Libraries.
8. Hogg, Patrick Scott, *Robert Burns: The Patriot Bard* (Edinburgh: Mainstream Publishing Company, 2008) p. 14.
9. Paterson, James, *History of the Counties of Ayr and Wigton* (Edinburgh: Stillie, 1864), p. 126.
10. Lawson, Reverend Roderick, *Place of Interest About Girvan with Glimpses of Carrick History* (Paisley: J and R Parlane, 1892), p. 33.
11. *ibid.*
12. Interview of author Tom Barclay.
13. *ibid.*
14. Cornwell and Hobbs, p. 49.
15. Truckell, A. E., *Dumfries and Galloway Traditions: Sawnie Bane (pamphlet on pile), Ewart Library, Dumfries.*

Chapter Eight

1. *The Invention of Tradition*, ed. by Eric Hobsbawn, Hugh Trevor Ranger, Hugh Trevor Roper, Prys Morgan, and David Cannadine (Cambridge: University of Cambridge Press, 1984), p. 15.

2. Saunie Bane, Ewart Library, Dumfries.
3. Truckell.
4. Lawson, p. 2.
5. *ibid.*, p. 3.
6. Deen, Ronald, *On The Trail of Sawney Bean and his Cannibal Family* (Glasgow: Tinel Printers, 1995), p. 1.
7. Cornwell and Hobbs, p. 54.

Chapter Nine

1. Campbell, Angus, *Scottish Tales of Terror* (London/Glasgow: Collins Fontana Books, 1972), p. 171.
2. Parish Records, General Register Office of Scotland.
3. *ibid.*
4. *ibid.*
5. *ibid.*
6. *ibid.*

Chapter Ten

1. Cross.
2. Cornwell and Hobbs, p. 52.
3. Robert Nye and Bill Watson, *Sawney Bean* (Bath: The Pitman Press, 1970), preface.
4. Morse, L. A., *The Flesh Eaters* (New York: Warner Books, 1979), preface.
5. Tait, Harry, *The Ballad of Sawney Bain* (Edinburgh: Polygon, 1990).
6. Gates, Frieda, *Sawney Beane: The Abduction of Elspeth Cumming* (Cambridge: Sterling & Ross, 2008).
7. Campbell, p. 171.
8. Sayers, Dorothy L., *Great Short Stories of Detection, Mystery and Horror* (London: Victor Gollancz, 1928), p. 1094.
9. Maine, C. E., *The World's Strangest Crimes* (New York: Pocket Edition Books, 1970), p. 30.
10. Colin Wilson and Patricia Pitman, *Encyclopedia of Murder* (London: Arthur Baker, 1961), p. 58.
11. *The Hills Have Eyes*, DVD Set, Disk 2 (Anchor Bay Entertainment, 1977), Special Features.
12. Interview of Natalie Rowan, Marketing Executive at the Edinburgh Dungeon, Merlin Entertainments Group.
13. Sylvanus Urban, 'Letter to the Editor', *The Gentleman's Magazine*, February 1829, p. 127.
14. Roughead, p. 89.
15. Holmes, p. 7.
16. Cornwell and Hobbs, p. 53.

Chapter Eleven

1. Gribble, p. 32.
2. 'Sawney Bean: Myth or Myth', p. 16.

3. Strawhoon, John, 'Ayrshire: The Story of a County' in *Ayrshire Historical Society* (Ayr: T. M. Gemmell & Sons, 1975), p. 17.
4. Strawhoon, p. 34.
5. Steven Brocklehurst, 'Who Was Sawney Bean?', 22 February 2013 (http://www.bbc.co.uk/news/uk-scotland-21506077).
6. 'Sawney Bean: Myth or Myth', p. 17.
7. Strawhoon, p. 38.

Chapter Twelve

1. Black, Fiona, *The Polar Twins* (Edinburgh: John Donald, 1999), p. 157.
2. 'Sawney Bean: Myth or Myth', p. 19.
3. Stephen Graham, 'The Legend of Sawney Bean', no date, (http://www.mysteriousbritain.co.uk/scotland/dumfriesshire/legends/the-legend-of-sawney-bean.html).

Bibliography

Books

Agnew, Andrew, *The Hereditary Sheriffs of Galloway* (Edinburgh: David Douglas, 1893)

Ashton, John, *Chap-Books of the Eighteenth Century*, (Piccadilly: Chatto And Windus, 1882)

Black, Fiona, *The Polar Twins* (Edinburgh: John Donald Publishers, 1999)

Black, Ray, *Cannibals and Evil Cult Killers: The Most Unthinkable and Heinous Crimes* (London: Little Brown, 2006)

Buckle, Henry Thomas, *History of Civilisation in England*, vol. 2 (New York: D. Appleton, 1864)

Campbell, Angus, *Scottish Tales of Terror* (London/Glasgow: Collins Fontana Books, 1972)

Chambers, Robert, *History of the Rebellion in Scotland in 1745, 1746* (London: W & R Chambers, 1869)

Cheviot, Andrew, *Proverbs, Proverbial Expressions And Popular Rhymes Of Scotland* (Edinburgh: Alexander Gardner, 1896)

Crockett, Samuel Rutherford, *The Grey Man* (Ayr: Macdonald and Sprout, 1977)

Cross, F. C., *Songs Duets and Choruses in the Semi-Comic Pantomime of Harlequinn Highlander, or Sawney Bean's Cave*, performed at the Jones's Royal Circus, 11 June 1798, from the National Library of Scotland

Deen, Ronald, *On The Trail of Sawney Bean and his Cannibal Family* (Glasgow: Tinel Printers, 1995)

Doubleday, H. Arthur., *The Works of William Shakespeare* (London: Chiswick Press, 1896)

Gates, Frieda, *Sawney Beane: The Abduction of Elspeth Cumming* (Cambridge: Sterling & Ross, 2008)

Giles, J. A., *Matthew Paris's English History From 1235 to 1273*, vol. 1 (London: Henry G. Bohn, 1852)

Gould MD, George and Walter L. Pyle, *Anomalies and Curiosities of Medicine* (Philadelphia: W. B. Saunders, 1900)

Gribble, Leonard, *More Famous Historical Mysteries* (London: Frederick Muller, 1972)

Hamilton, Judy, *Scottish Murders* (New Lanark: Geddes & Grosset, 2001)

Harness, Reverend W. *Shakespeare's Dramatic Works,* Love's Labour Lost, Act II, Scene I (London: J. F. Dove, 1830)

Hobsbawn, Eric, Hugh Trevor Ranger, Hugh Trevor Roper, Prys Morgan, and David Cannadine (eds), *The Invention of Tradition* (Cambridge: University of Cambridge Press, 1984)

Hogg, Patrick Scott, *Robert Burns: The Patriot Bard* (Edinburgh: Mainstream, 2008)

Holmes, Ronald, *The Legend of Sawney Bean* (London: Mews, 1975)

Jackson, Henry, *Robinson Crusoe Social Engineer, How the discovery of Robinson Crusoe solves the labor problem and opens the path to industrial peace* (New York: E. P. Button and Company, 1922)

Johnson, Captain Charles, *A General and True History of the Lives and Actions Of the Most Famous Highwaymen, Murderers, Street-Robbers, &c. To Which is Added, A Genuine Account of the Voyages and Plunders, Of the Most Noted Pirates. Interspersed with several remarkable Tryals Of the Most Notorious Malefactors ... at the Sessions-House in the Old Baily, London. Adorn'd with the Effigies, and Other Material Transactions of the Most Remarkable Offenders, Engraved on Copper Plates* (Birmingham: R. L. Walker, 1742)

Kerman, Sandra Lee, *The Newgate Calendar or Malefactor's Bloody Register* (New York: Capricorn, 1962)

Lamont-Brown, Raymond, *Scottish Folklore* (Edinburgh: Birlinn, 1996)

Lang, Andrew W., *A Short History of Scotland* (London: Andrew Lang, 1911)

Lang, Theo, *The Queen's Scotland—Glasgow, Kyle and Galloway* (London: Hodder and Stoughton, 1953)

Lawson, Reverend Roderick, *Place of Interest About Girvan with Glimpses of Carrick History* (Paisley: J and R Parlane, 1892)

Love, Dane, *Legendary Ayrshire, Custom, Folklore, Tradition* (Ayr: Carn, 2009)

MacDiarmid, Hugh, *The Scottish Eccentrics* (London: George Routledge & Sons, 1936)

MacKay, Charles and Allan G. May Ramsay, *A Dictionary of Lowland Scotch* (Boston: Ticknor, 1888)

Mackay, John, *Cannibal Family of Sawney Bean and Stories of South West Scotland* (Glasgow: Lang Syne, 2007)

Mackenzie, Ross, *Culloden, The Swords and the Sorrows* (Glasgow: The National Trust for Scotland Trading Company, 1996)

Mackenzie, William, *History of Galloway From the Earliest Time to the Present*, vol. 1 (Kirkcudbright: John Nicholson, 1841)

Macleod, Innes F., *Where the Whaups Are Crying: A Dumfries and Galloway Anthology* (Glasgow: Birlinn, 2001)

Maine, C. E., *The World's Strangest Crimes* (New York: Pocket Edition Books, 1970)

Maxwell, Sir Herbert, *A History of Dumfries and Galloway* (Edinburgh: William Blackwood and Sons, 1896)

McLachlan, Malcolm, *Rambles in Galloway: Topographical, and Biographical* (Edinburgh: Edmonston & Douglas, 1876)

McMahon, Vanessa, *Murder in Shakespeare's England* (London: Hambledon & London, 2004)

Bibliography

M'Kerlie, R.S.A. SCOT. F.R.G.S. etc., P. H., *History of the Lands and Their Owners In Galloway With Historical Sketches of the District*, vol. 2 (London: Simpkin, Marshall, Hamilton, Kent & Co. LMD, 1906)

Morse, L. A., *The Flesh Eaters* (New York: Warner Books, 1979)

Nicholson, John, *Historical and Traditional Tales in Prose and Verse Connected With the South of Scotland* (Kirkcudbright: John Nicholson, 1843)

Nye, Robert and Bill Watson, *Sawney Bean* (Bath: The Pitman Press, 1970)

Ó Danachair, Donal (ed.), *The Newgate Calendar,* vol. 1 (The Ex-Classics Project, 2009) (http://www.exclassics.com/newgate/ng01.pdf)

Paterson, James, *History of the Counties of Ayr and Wigton* (Edinburgh: Stillie, 1864)

Pittock, Murray G. H., *The Myth of the Jacobite Clans* (Edinburgh: Edinburgh University Press, 1999)

Holinshed, Raphael, *Scottish Chronicle: A Complete History and Description of Scotland*, vol. 1 (Glasgow: A. Wilson, 1805)

Robertson, William, *Historical Tales and Legends of Ayrshire* (London: Himilton, Adams and Co., 1889)

Roughead, William, *Rogues Walk Here* (London: Cassell, 1934)

Sayers, Dorothy L., *Great Short Stories of Detection, Mystery and Horror* (London: Victor Gollancz, 1928)

Tait, Harry, *The Ballad of Sawney Bain* (Edinburgh: Polygon, 1990)

Tolkien, J. R. R., *The Fellowship of the Ring,* (New York: Ballantine Books, 1976)

The Official Scrabble Player's Dictionary, 4th ed. (New York: Merriam-Webster, 2005)

The Terrific Register—or Record of Crimes, Judgments, Providences and Calamities, vol. 1 (London: Sherwood, Jones, and Co., 1825)

Van der Kiste, John, *William and Mary* (London: The History Press, 2003)

Colin Wilson and Patricia Pitman, *Encyclopedia of Murder* (London: Arthur Baker, 1961)

Wood, J. Maxwell, *Witchcraft in South-West Scotland* (Dumfries: EP, 1975)

Periodicals

Fiona Armstrong, 'Dumfries & Galloway', *Scotland Magazine*, 2, June 2002.

Bernard Capp, 'Serial Killers in 17th Century England', *HistoryToday*, 46.3 (1996), (http://www.historytoday.com/story/13835). Peter Christie, 'The True Story of the North Devon Savages', *Transactions of the Devonshire Association*, 124, December 1992.

David Cornwell and Sandy Hobbs, 'Sawney Bean, the Scottish Cannibal', *Folklore*, 108 (1997).

R.S. Ferguson, 'On the Collection of Chap-books in the Bibliotheca Jacksoniana, in Tullie House, Carlisle, with some remarks on the History of Printing in Carlisle, Whitehaven, Penrith and other north country towns', *Transactions of the Cumberland and Westmoreland Antiquarian and Archeological Society*, 14 (1897).

'Sawney Bean: Myth or Myth', *Ayrshire Notes*, 23, Autumn 2002.

John Strawhoon, 'Ayrshire: The Story of a County' in *Ayrshire Historical Society* (Ayr: T. M. Gemmell & Sons, 1975).

The London Quarterly Review, October 1896 to January 1897 (London: C. H. Kelly, 1897).

Timothy Taylor, 'The Edible Dead', *British Archeology*, 59, June 2001 (http://www.archaeologyuk.org/ba/ba59/feat1.shtml).

Sylvanus Urban, 'Letter to the Editor', *The Gentleman's Magazine*, February 1829.

Newspapers

Steven Brocklehurst, 'Who Was Sawney Bean?', 22 February 2013 (http://www.bbc.co.uk/news/uk-scotland-21506077).

'Sawney just loved baked human beans', *The Sun*, 12 September 1994. p.E1

Robin McKie, 'Bones from a Cheddar Gorge cave show that cannibalism helped Britain's earliest settlers survive the ice age', 20 June 2010, (http://www.theguardian.com/science/2010/jun/20/ice-age-cannibals-britain-earliest-settlers).

Archives

Carricta Meridionalis Map of South Carrick, South Ayshire Libraries.
Parish Records, General Register Office of Scotland.
Special Collections, National Library of Scotland.
The History of Sawney Beane and his Family, robbers and murderers, etc. Author: Sawney Beane (Birmingham: S. & T. Martin, 1810).
Truckell, A. E., *Dumfries and Galloway Traditions: Sawnie Bane* (pamphlet on pile), Ewart Library, Dumfries.

Other

The Hills Have Eyes, Special DVD Edition.
Stephen Graham, 'The Legend of Sawney Bean' (http://www.mysteriousbritain.co.uk/scotland/dumfriesshire/legends/the-legend-of-sawney-bean.html).